Curriculum Leadership

Case Studies
for Program
Practitioners

Association for Supervision
and Curriculum Development
Alexandria, Virginia

David S. Martin
with
Allan Glatthorn,
Marilyn Winters,
and Philip Saif

. . . Organizing principles [in curriculum] include: . . . the use of description followed by analysis, the development of specific illustrations followed by broader and broader principles to explain these illustrations. . . .

RALPH W. TYLER
in *Basic Principles of Curriculum*
University of Chicago Press, 1949

ASCD publications present a variety of viewpoints. The views expressed or implied in this publication are not necessarily official positions of the Association.

Printed in the United States of America.

Ronald S. Brandt, ASCD Executive Editor
Nancy Carter Modrak, Managing Editor, Books
Al Way, Manager, Design Services

ASCD Stock No. 611-89013
Typeset by Mid-Atlantic Photo Composition, Inc.
Printed by St. Mary's Press
$12.95

Library of Congress Cataloging-in-Publication Data

Curriculum leadership.

1. Curriculum planning—United States—Case studies. 2. School management and organization—United States—Case studies. I. Martin, David S.
LB2806.15.C86   1989   375'.001'0973   88-33306
ISBN 0-87120-155-0

Curriculum Leadership:

Case Studies for Program Practitioners

Foreword

Inquiry begins with a problem focus—a discrepant event, a dilemma, or a perplexing situation requiring resolution. In this volume, we are presented with a collection of invitations for curriculum inquiry. The 22 case studies provide a rich array of intriguing, real-life-in-schools controversies that will provoke philosophical and pragmatic dialogue among students and practitioners of curriculum.

This volume also reveals some parallel issues that illuminate the vast range and scope of the curriculum worker. It defines the professional role of the curriculum decision maker as complex, rigorous, and skillful. It elevates curriculum inquiry as a respectable, professional discipline, demanding influential, intelligent, creative, and compassionate leadership.

The problems presented here demonstrate the interrelatedness of curriculum decision making and problem solving with all the other areas of the educational system: finances, personnel, staff development, community relations, evaluation and research, and political action. It makes abundantly clear that curriculum leaders must be well grounded in human relations skills; they must command the ability to plan carefully and to communicate precisely. They must possess a well-articulated set of philosophical beliefs and a clear vision of the desired state of the educational enterprise. Furthermore, they must have the personal security and stamina to face the staggering enigmas of their chosen field.

Once again, ASCD makes a proud contribution to the professional development of the curriculum leader. Authors Glatthorn, Martin, Saif, and Winters have selected their case studies to illustrate the range and variety of decisions that challenge the curriculum worker. The questions they pose at the conclusion of each case will tease the curious, spur the entrenched to reconsider alternatives, and encourage all involved to become more empathetic in their consideration of others' points of view. These questions will no doubt result in heated debate, controversial dialogue, and the generation of further questions. Ultimately, what this volume offers to the involved reader is a heightened awareness of curriculum issues and the impetus to apply the learnings from these case studies to the everyday situations in which professional educators struggle to improve their schools' curricular offerings, enhance student learning, align their philosophy and practice, and create a better world through education.

ARTHUR L. COSTA
ASCD President,
1988-89

Introduction and Model for Case Analyses

Textbooks and other printed materials are widely available today on the theory and practice of curriculum development and management in schools. Many of these books provide interesting presentations of concepts along with examples of their applications. However, most large texts, which must present both curriculum theory and administrative procedures, do not provide detailed case studies. As a result, there has been a clear need for a supplementary text that provides students of curriculum and practicing leaders within the field an in-depth opportunity to apply these concepts to real cases drawn from practice in educational institutions. That is what this book does; it presents cases based on actual events in a variety of settings to help readers think about and plan appropriate ways to manage problems and situations typical in curriculum practice today. Thus, this book is designed to fill an important need in the preservice and inservice training of curriculum leaders.

Organization of the Book

We have grouped our 22 case studies according to five themes: (1) curriculum decision-making, (2) curriculum implementation, (3) issues in personnel and curriculum, (4) programs for special populations, and (5) curriculum evaluation.

Each case study describes a situation actually experienced by one or more curriculum leaders—for instance, responding to parent objections about classroom materials; taking the initiative in improving student test scores; revising curriculum to meet the needs of special populations; resolving the dilemma of who owns the curriculum—administrators, teachers, or the community; and coping with the need to reduce expenditures without damaging the core of the curriculum.[1]

A Model for Case Analysis

Each case study includes a brief description of the setting (the school environment, demographics of the region), a narrative of the events and actions of the various individuals and constituencies, and a list of questions that focus on key issues in the case.

The cases do *not* offer solutions; the reader is not told the ultimate solution in the actual case or given suggestions for possible solutions. There are two reasons for this deliberate omission. First, the *process* of wrestling with the issues is as important as the actual outcomes, and many readers may well derive better solutions than those applied in the real situations. Second, the easy presence of a solution could well short-cut that process for the eager reader.

The most appropriate model for analyzing these cases would follow a particular sequence of input, processing, and output. We encourage readers to follow these steps:

1. Try to list three or four underlying issues that seem to be at the heart of the case.

2. Working alone or with a study group or partner, propose a set of two or three different solution directions. You need to consider the entire setting of the case and apply whatever you have already learned from the curriculum field.

3. In proposing a course of action, be prepared to present a rationale. You should draw from several sources: well-grounded curriculum theories, empirical research, experts' recommendations for practice, and reflections about your own experience.

4. Either alone or with partners, list several possible consequences for each of your proposed actions. Be sure to consider the nature of the principal "players" and constituencies when you generate these consequences.

5. Rank your proposals from "most likely to succeed" to "least likely to succeed."

6. Prepare a short presentation of your best or "most likely to succeed" solution, and include the particular principles you relied

---

[1] Although the case studies in this book are based on actual events and situations, the names of communities, school districts, and individuals have been changed to ensure anonymity. Any similarity to existing locations and individuals is purely coincidental.

upon in making that selection. Be prepared to defend your solution when you present it.

By following this procedure, you will find yourself easily moving into the mode of a curriculum decision-maker who takes advantage of prior experience, theory, and careful practical thinking in order to create an action plan that is the most appropriate for the situation.

The title "curriculum director" appears frequently in the text to refer to the person whose point of view the reader is expected to take in devising courses of action. We recognize that that title is not found in many school systems; we use it here to refer to any school professional who has direct responsibility for curriculum or instructional leadership: curriculum coordinator, assistant/associate superintendent for instruction, director of programs, and the like.

A Word About the Authors

The authors of this text have among them many years of experience in leading curriculum development in school settings as well as in teaching *about* curriculum at the university level and in preparing curriculum specialists. Nonetheless, each author would be quick to admit that many, perhaps all, of the case studies in this book have no single best solution. Most have several better or worse solutions that vary according to the circumstances, the style of the leader, and numerous intangible factors such as timing and the composition of the particular leadership in the community at the time of the case events.

David S. Martin, Dean of the School of Education and Human Services and Professor of Education at Gallaudet University, spent 10 years as a director of curriculum in two public school districts (one on the East Coast and one on the West) and has taught courses in curriculum leadership for several years at the undergraduate and graduate levels. He has also provided workshops for inservice curriculum leaders in school districts throughout the country.

Philip S. Saif is Affiliate Professor of Education at George Mason University in Fairfax, Virginia. He has been a director of curriculum and evaluation, a coordinator of research development and evaluation, and a director of research and planning. He has served extensively as an educational consultant in several Middle Eastern countries.

Marilyn Winters is Associate Professor in the Department of Educational Administration at California State University in Sacramento. She has long experience in the roles of director of instruction, curriculum specialist, and school administrator. She is active in several professional curriculum organizations and is the author of *Preparing Your Curriculum Guide* (Association for Supervision and Curriculum Development).

As coordinator of a cooperative doctoral program, **Allan Glatthorn** holds a joint appointment as Professor at East Carolina University and Visiting Professor at North Carolina State University. He was formerly chair of the Educational Leadership Division at the Graduate School of Education of the University of Pennsylvania; he has been a high school principal, curriculum coordinator, and classroom teacher. He is the author of two recent books on curriculum and has consulted with numerous school districts in their curriculum revision projects.

The authors express their appreciation to Janis Bouck of Gallaudet University for valuable revisions and additions from the sender's point of view, and to Alice Drew and Mary Butler, also of Gallaudet University, for word processing preparation of the manuscript.

Group I.
Cases in
Curriculum
Decision Making

In this section we have five cases relating to the development and adoption of a districtwide curriculum and to how administrators, teachers, and the local community affect the development process. How much power does the director of curriculum actually have, and what would you do, if you were in that position, to ensure that education in the district is on the best possible track?

Case Study 1

The School Board and Curriculum from the Top Down

Issue: Authority of administration

The small city of Elizabeth, Rhode Island, was a former industrial community with one major factory still operating. The population had the full range of socioeconomic levels, including a large blue-collar segment that had lived in the city for three generations.

The school district had 8,000 K-12 students. Thirteen elementary schools fed into two junior high schools, a comprehensive high school, and a vocational high school. The nine-member school board was elected by the general population. (Five members of the current board graduated from the high school in the city and remembered their school days with some fondness.) The director of curriculum, George Gresham, reported directly to the superintendent of schools, who also had an assistant superintendent for personnel.

The district required all proposals for curriculum change to pass through a series of channels, starting at the school level and proceeding upward to a curriculum council (representing all schools and departments in the district), the superintendent, and a subcommittee on curriculum of the school board, which could then recommend it to the full school board.

Until recently, the high school social studies curriculum followed a traditional format: a required course in world history, usually taken in the freshman or sophomore year; a required year of American history; and a senior year course called Principles of Citizenship.

Gresham, together with a committee of social studies teachers at the high school, recently developed a proposal for two elective options as alternatives to the requirement in world history. One elective was a world civilization course, which emphasized ideas from the arts in several major historical periods as well as the history of ideas, as opposed to the political and military emphasis of the current world history course. This elective was designed in particular to challenge the more able learner. The second elective option was a world cultures course, which provided an anthropological study of seven world cultures, including three non-Western cultures, and was designed to appeal to the general high school population.

Both course proposals were well developed and included specific objectives, a variety of teaching materials, and a balance of classroom activities.

After these proposals passed through the curriculum council, Gresham discussed them with the superintendent, who made it clear that she favored maintaining the current organization of the high school curriculum, which provided a central focus for all students.

Gresham then brought the proposals to a meeting of the school board's subcommittee on curriculum. The subcommittee praised Gresham's efforts to bring new ideas forward, but it did not actually endorse his proposals. Gresham then explained that the rationale behind them was to provide alternative learning paths for different students in the school and to bring ideas from social sciences other than history and geography into the social studies curriculum.

One subcommittee member responded, "I worry very much that students taking either of these new courses would not have the facts about important events in world history that we all had in high school."

Another member said, "I suppose the subject matter of these courses would be interesting, but history and geography must continue to be the core of the social studies program."

The subcommittee chair then asked for the superintendent's opinion. She replied, "When I discussed this proposal with the director of curriculum, I mentioned that I thought he needed to do more homework on the proposal. There isn't enough support from the research to back up these ideas, and I think that what we've used these many years has served our students well. After all, each year a number of our students get into some of the best colleges, and many of our students find good jobs. I'm not at all convinced that this is an appropriate proposal, and I think it needs more study."

The chair of the subcommittee then turned to Gresham and said, "Well, I suppose we could bring this to the full board meeting, but it would not have a recommendation from this subcommittee, and

I'm sure that the feelings of the other board members would be as strong as ours here. Since we don't want to take a negative vote right now, I suggest that you take the proposal back for some additional consideration. Thank you very much for bringing it to us."

The meeting concluded, and Gresham began thinking about appropriate steps for the following day, when he would need to contact members of the social studies faculty who had worked on the proposal.

Discussion Questions

1. What were the underlying issues behind this temporary failure for the curriculum leader?

2. Where did the decision-making authority in the school district truly reside in matters of curriculum?

3. What steps should the director of curriculum take the following morning?

4. What should he tell the members of the social studies faculty who had worked on the proposal?

5. What should he do differently in the future when he proposes a change in other subject fields?

Case Study 2

Teachers' Power in Deciding Curriculum

Issue: Role of teachers in deciding curriculum

Suburban Chester, Oregon, had a preponderence of professional families and a significant minority population that led alternative lifestyles characterized by communal living, low-income vocations in the arts, and ultra-left political views. There was a relatively high proportion of single-parent families, although quite a few children attended private schools. The public school system consisted of seven elementary schools that fed into a single middle school of grades 6-8. That school, in turn, fed into a high school that was part of a different secondary school district. Parents in the community had traditionally played a leading role in decisions about school programs and directions, and a number of the teachers appeared to be allied with parents in demanding a variety of educational alternatives.

The director of curriculum, Shelby Coles, reported directly to the superintendent of schools, and over the past two years had developed numerous district-level subject matter curriculum committees, including a social studies committee, an English committee, a kindergarten committee, and others. Each committee was chaired by a teacher who consulted regularly with Coles. The committees were charged with (1) analyzing the status of the specific curriculum area in each school, (2) developing new or revised curriculum guides for use by all teachers in the district in that subject, and (3) recommending these curriculum guides to the superintendent through Shelby, who would then bring them before the school board for an adoption decision. The school board consisted of five elected members, each representing a different segment of this rather diverse community.

During the past year, the English Curriculum Committee, which included six teachers from both middle school and elementary levels, had produced a proposed new curriculum guide for grades K-8. Committee members met biweekly for two hours throughout the year to write and revise a list of sequenced objectives; a list of appropriate types of activities for teachers to select from; a list of recommended materials for teaching spelling, writing, reading, and literature; and some possible evaluation strategies that teachers could use to assess the achievement of their students. The guide was circulated to all teachers three weeks before the school board meeting. The superintendent was enthusiastic about the proposed curriculum because it seemed to provide a level of coordination that the English program had lacked.

As usual, the school board meeting was well attended by at least 50 members of the public and some members of the school professional staff. When the meeting convened, Shelby Coles was invited to explain the purpose and background of the new curriculum guide. She began by introducing members of the curriculum committee who were in the audience, and completed her presentation by asking the board members for questions. Several board members were obviously pleased that the curriculum "finally" coordinated the district's English programs and stated that they hoped similar kinds of products would be forthcoming in other subject areas.

The chair of the school board then turned to the superintendent for his recommendation. He replied by praising the members of the committee and the director of curriculum and endorsing the adoption. The chair of the board then turned to the audience, as was always done in this community, to ask if there were any questions or comments. A parent stood to be recognized and expressed her positive feeling that this curriculum was a forward step. In addition, she hoped that it would be *followed* and not ignored by the teachers in the district. A short silence ensued, and then three teachers in the audience asked to be recognized. None of these teachers were members of the English Curriculum Committee.

The first teacher stood and said, "I know that the committee worked hard on this program, but we in the teacher group feel that we did not have sufficient time to react to the proposal." The second teacher said, "The feeling among the teachers is much stronger than that just expressed by my colleague; in fact, as an officer of the Teachers' Association, I would like to register a formal protest that the prescription of curriculum should not be made at the district administrative level. It is, instead, the prerogative of every teacher to determine the curriculum that best fits the needs of the children in the class." This statement was obviously written in advance; while Coles was surprised at the response (as was the superintendent), it was clear that there had been a prior meeting of Teacher Association officers before the school board meeting. The third teacher stood to be recognized and supported the statement made by the second teacher.

The chair of the school board, apparently taken aback, kept his composure and asked if there were other comments. When no one spoke up, he turned to Coles and asked for a reply to these comments before the board took any action.

Discussion Questions

1. What specific issues underlie this case in relation to the curriculum development process?

2. What steps should the superintendent take to determine to what extent the opposing teachers' statements represent the teachers as a whole? (*Were* these teachers representative, or were they a small subgroup?)

3. In what way should the director of curriculum reply to the chair of the school board? What should Shelby Coles say now, and what should she promise to report on later?

4. What might the director of curriculum do differently in the future when developing new curriculums for other subject areas?

Case Study 3

The Parents' Association and the Curriculum Agenda

Issue: Community effects on the curriculum

The town of Jeffrey, Kansas, had 15,000 residents who depended heavily on the wheat-growing business. Three years ago a new superintendent of schools, Lester Macomb, was hired from the Chicago area. During the past year he asked his school principals to institute a program of sex and AIDS education in the upper elementary and junior high grades.

Citing trends in the expansion of sex and AIDS education in many school systems around the country, Macomb provided the schools with additional funds to purchase published materials, including books, filmstrips, and videos. Taking a "low-key" approach, he gave relatively little publicity to the new program; he simply informed the school board last year that the program was being instituted. As the program moved into its second year, however, at least 18 parents complained that the topic of sex and AIDS education was inappropriate for the school to include in its curriculum. In each case, the concern was registered first with the classroom teacher, who referred it to the school principal. And in each case the principal defended the importance of sex and AIDS education because of its centrality to a well-informed public. Until recently, no specific complaint had been addressed to either the school board or to Macomb's office; however, the principals had kept him informed about the complaints.

For a month, there were no complaints at all. Then, one night as Macomb worked late preparing for the next school board meeting in nine days, he opened a letter from the president of the Jeffrey

Parent-Teachers Association. It was a two-page communication from Mrs. Betty Edgewood, whom Macomb had met at PTA social functions but with whom he had not discussed school programs in great depth.

The letter officially expressed concern on the part of the board of the Jeffrey PTA regarding the inclusion of sex and AIDS education without consulting parents and without giving parents an opportunity to have a *choice* in the matter. The letter further referred to an agreement made 20 years earlier by a group of clergy in the community that "family life education" would be included as a part of the religious education curriculum in each of Jeffrey's four churches. Mrs. Edgewood's letter demanded that the superintendent immediately withdraw the curriculum from school programs and requested a discussion at the next meeting of the school board. The letter was copied to the chair of the school board.

The next day Superintendent Macomb called a special meeting of the school principals and asked each to present what he or she knew of the background of the complaint, as well as recommendations on appropriate action for the school district.

The principals of the three elementary schools said they were aware that the local PTA boards were discussing the concern, but they thought the focus of those discussions had been on having more time in the curriculum for reading and mathematics since state test scores for the district had shown no significant improvement in those areas over the past five years. The principal of the junior high school recalled hearing two parent officers of the school association complain that their children were conversing "far too freely" about sex. Th ` high school principal had heard several parents worry about the increase over the last two years in teenage pregnancy throughout the state as well as in Jeffrey.

During the meeting, Macomb was interrupted by a call from the chair of the school board, who had just received his copy of Mrs. Edgewood's letter. Macomb and the chair decided to place the item on the school board agenda, and the chair agreed to call Mrs. Edgewood to let her know.

On the evening of the school board meeting, Mrs. Edgewood presented a summary of her letter and added statistics relating to reading and mathematics test scores from the past two years and emphasized that the time being spent on sex and AIDS education would be better served by focusing on reading and mathematics instruction. She concluded her remarks by emphasizing that sex and AIDS education was the province of the home and the church.

When Mrs. Edgewood took her seat, Rev. Brown from one of the local churches stood to speak. He pointed out that sex and AIDS education in the schools was apparently encouraging teenagers throughout the country to experiment more with sex, as evidenced by the increase in teenage pregnancy, even in Jeffrey. Rev. Brown reiterated that sex and AIDS education remained a part of the 11th grade curriculum in the religious education course in his church.

Following Rev. Brown's remarks, the chair of the school board turned to the superintendent and asked what action he would take on this request.

Discussion Questions

1. What are the *real* issues in this case?

2. Suppose that Superintendent Macomb had asked the director of curriculum to advise him before the meeting about what he should say at the end of Mrs. Edgewood's remarks. What should the director have told the superintendent?

3. How should Macomb, at the school board meeting, respond to the issue of test scores in reading and mathematics? How should he reply to Mrs. Edgewood and Rev. Brown?

4. If you were a teacher in this school district and heard about this issue on the day following the school board meeting, what would be your response?

5. Suppose that Macomb asked the curriculum director to immediately form a districtwide committee to study this question; what persons representing which constituencies should form the membership of this committee, and what activities should be on their agenda?

6. Or suppose, instead, that Macomb were to ask the principals to get together with him on the morning following the school board meeting. What plan of action would you recommend the superin-

tendent take during the two weeks before the next school board meeting, when he is to make a progress report on this request?

6. Should the superintendent and director of curriculum have acted differently at the beginning? How?

Case Study 4

The State and the Local District

Issue: Control of the curriculum

The Hereford County School System served several rural communities in a Southeastern state. It had a relatively small pupil population: approximately 4,500 students attended the two high schools and eight elementary schools, serving grades K-8, which were scattered around the county. The school system had a small central office staff. The director of curriculum, Sandra Allen, coordinated the program for exceptional children and aspired to the position of superintendent since the current superintendent, Harold Sampson, was approaching retirement. Allen believed she could improve her chances for advancement by playing a strong leadership role in coordinating the school system's curriculum.

Smithville School was one of the small elementary schools in the Hereford County system. Its principal, Walker Thompson, was an energetic leader who prided himself on both knowing the community and being in the forefront of educational change. He served a community that had been in a slow decline for years; most of the adults worked for minimum wage in semiskilled and unskilled jobs. Even though most of the community seemed to hold rather conservative views about both politics and education, they valued Thompson because of his close involvement with the people and his concern for quality education. Thompson also aspired to be superintendent; he was confident that he was the most qualified and enjoyed the greatest support. He was aware of Allen's ambitions but didn't consider her to be a serious competitor. He was active in professional associations and had published two journal articles about his school and its innovative middle school curriculum.

There were 18 professionals on the Smithville faculty, all experienced teachers who had grown up in the region and who liked the children. The teachers assigned to the middle grades supported Thompson wholeheartedly, since he had made sure they received more than their share of resources. Most of the K-5 teachers, however, were lukewarm toward him. They recognized his leadership skills but at times resented the special attention he gave to the middle school teachers and their program. The K-5 teachers also had more conservative educational views and among themselves complained about the middle school program.

That program was an interdisciplinary science and humanities program for grades 6-8. Middle school teachers with backgrounds in language arts, social studies, and science had organized themselves into interdisciplinary teams. In recent years they had developed what seemed to be an exciting interdisciplinary curriculum that focused on the traditions and problems of the local region. Students spent much of their time doing field work in the community; under the teachers' direction, they conducted their own investigations into local dialects, old customs and folkways, and community problems.

Two years earlier, in an effort to upgrade the quality of the state's schools, the state legislature had enacted legislation requiring its Department of Education to develop and implement competency-based "standard courses of study" for all public schools. The state curriculum office organized committees, held public hearings, and then produced the required curriculum guides for each major subject area. Most independent curriculum experts who reviewed the guides considered them to be of only average quality and their design and approach to be somewhat conventional. The English/language arts guide, for example, included some content that reflected current approaches in the field, such as an emphasis on the writing process and media analysis, but it also stressed traditional grammar and punctuation.

In responding to a legislative testing mandate, the Department had recently announced plans to develop and administer competency tests, based on the state guides, in all areas of the curriculum.

In early August, Sandra Allen conducted a curriculum workshop for the principals in the county. She reviewed the state's new curriculum regulations, distributed copies of the guides for the standard courses of study, praised the guides for their quality, and announced her plans to work with teachers in each school to translate the guides into unit and daily lesson plans. For most of the workshop, Principal Walker Thompson remained quiet—but was obviously upset. As the workshop drew to a close, he spoke at length and with conviction, attacking the "heavy hand of the state" and ridiculing the quality of the guides. He was especially vehement in criticizing the content and approach for the middle grades, noting that in his view, his middle school curriculum was clearly superior to that reflected in the new state guides. He concluded with a sarcastic comment about "central office administrators who don't know what's going on in the schools." Allen made a conciliatory comment, so as to adjourn the meeting without further conflict. However, she deeply resented his public attack.

After the meeting adjourned, she asked Thompson to discuss the issue further in her office. Again she began by trying to mollify him. She praised his program and assured him that the new state guides would not interfere with his innovative middle school curriculum. She pointed out that the state competencies in language arts, social studies, and science could easily be integrated into an interdisciplinary approach. Thompson was not convinced. He argued that the rather traditional content of most of the state guides was in direct conflict with the goals of his program. "I want the kids studying the local dialect, not hunting for participles," he said. Allen felt herself becoming combative. She reminded him that curriculum was not determined at the school level, noted the authority of the state legislature, and pointed out that the new state tests might make the whole issue moot anyway.

In an attempt to resolve the issue without further controversy, Allen asked if she could meet with Thompson and his faculty during the county's inservice days to be held during the last week of August. Thompson reluctantly agreed. Allen would meet with him and his teachers on the second inservice day; he would spend the first day working with his own staff.

Following that confrontation, Allen conferred with Superintendent Sampson. She painted a rather negative picture of Thompson, casting him as a "prima donna" who "always wanted to have his own way." Sampson, who at times seemed a bit jealous of Thompson's professional success, gave Allen his strong support. "You be sure to let Thompson know that there is no choice—he will use the state guides. I'm getting a little tired of that Mickey Mouse middle school program anyway."

During the first inservice day when Thompson met with his staff, he devoted a great deal of time to attacking the state guides. He strongly praised all that the teachers had accomplished and told them that implementing the new guides would undermine their entire program. He cast the issue in personal terms, stressing his hope that the faculty would support him in this current conflict.

One of the middle school teachers proposed that faculty members sign a petition supporting Thompson and appealing for an exemption from the state's new curriculum requirements. A few of the K-5 teachers demurred. While they were obviously reluctant to incur Thompson's wrath, a few were secretly pleased that the much-touted middle school program might be supplanted by a more conventional curriculum. Sensing that he did not have the unqualified support of his faculty, Thompson suggested that they should adopt a wait-and-see attitude. They would meet with Allen on the following day, see what she had to say, and then make up their minds as to what they should do.

Discussion Questions

1. What do you see as the central education issue in this conflict?

2. How do you think that issue should be resolved? What theory and research do you believe would support your position?

3. If you were Allen, what would be your general strategy in meeting with Thompson and the faculty? What would your long-term goal be? What would you attempt to accomplish in that meeting to advance you toward that goal? How would you plan to deal with Thompson?

4. If you were Thompson, what would your general strategy be? What would be your long-term goal and short-term objectives? What would you hope to accomplish in the meeting? How would you plan to deal with Allen?

5. How do you think the superintendent should deal with the conflict between Allen and Thompson? Why?

Case Study 5

Professional and Community Factions Around Instructional Methods

Issue: Philosophical conflict among teachers

Belton, Ohio, was a middle- to upper-middle-class suburb of a large industrial city. More than half the parents in the school community had a college education, and many were involved in professional or creative work. The elected school board was composed of one housewife, two lawyers, a professor, and an engineer; all were or had been parents of students in the school district.

Approximately half the families in the district believed the schools should provide an *open* opportunity for their children to explore their own interests and not be bound by traditional teaching methods. The other half were either content to let the school decide what was best for their children or believed strongly in the values of a strict traditional education with firm classroom discipline and regular measurement of their children's progress on national and state standardized tests. The philosophies and teaching methods of the teachers working in the district roughly reflected the different philosophies of the parents. This similarity was intentional, the result of a balanced-hiring policy designed to provide a teaching corps as diverse as the community.

Over the past two years some parents and educators had felt a growing need to re-examine and update the social studies curriculum. The school board had recently asked the superintendent, Mary

Kelly, to move forward in decisions about new social studies text materials for the district, since the cycle of state adoption of textbooks that year focused on social studies. Kelly responded by asking the principals of all the elementary and secondary schools to appoint one or more teachers to a districtwide Social Studies Materials Committee.

At the committee's first meeting, Kelly asked the committee to recommend, within three months, a single text program, to be purchased with state funds, that would unite the K-12 social studies curriculum with a common program and theme. At the second meeting, the committee selected a chair, and the director of curriculum, Dwayne Hayes, joined as an ex-officio member. Hayes brought to the meeting several samples of the eight major published programs from which the committee could choose a recommended text.

At the committee's third meeting, the chair suggested (on Hayes' advice) that before undertaking any selection or review, the committee agree on some general criteria for the most desirable program for the district. In the ensuing discussion, five of the ten committee members expressed strong convictions that the adopted program should (1) follow a careful sequence of history from past to present; (2) begin with the study of the home, then the community, and outward to the world at large; and (3) teach children particular moral values connected with being honest and productive citizens in the most important nation on earth.

Four of the remaining five members expressed equally strong convictions that any social studies program chosen should (1) permit children to study other cultures from an early age; (2) provide moral dilemmas in which children could make decisions based on their own set of values, which they would be free to express; (3) allow children to select from a wide range of choices within any given social studies topic; and (4) present a strong focus on current social issues, including the importance of banning nuclear testing and the removal of United States investments in South Africa.

The remaining member of the committee finally said, "Well, it seems that once again in this district we're going to go through all of this deep division of our views of what education should be. It's no wonder that some parents prefer to send their children to private schools when they see we can't get our act together in a coordinated plan. If I had the money, I'd do the same thing, but I only earn a teacher's salary, so I have to send my two kids to the public schools myself."

The committee chair suggested that perhaps the committee should include representatives from the parent community to help make sure the decision reflected their desires as well. He turned to Curriculum Director Hayes and asked, "Where do you believe we should proceed next in developing our criteria? Should we wait until the next meeting? I'm not sure we're ever going to reach consensus on this committee."

Only two months remained for making a decision.

Discussion Questions

1. What are the *real* curriculum issues in this case?

2. How should the director of curriculum respond to the specific question from the committee chair, and why?

3. What would be the advantages and disadvantages of involving parents in the work of the Social Studies Materials Committee at this point?

4. If the curriculum director instead of the superintendent had been developing the process for making a decision about the curriculum, should he have appointed such a committee? Why?

5. Since the committee already existed, how should the director involve the members in the selection process at this point?

6. What is a defensible view of the purpose of the social studies curriculum in a community as diverse as this one?

7. How can this view be applied to the plan of action?

8. What plan of action would you recommend for the committee's work over the next two months as the curriculum director confers with the chair? Be sure to state the rationale for each part of the plan.

Group II.
Cases in
Curriculum
Implementation

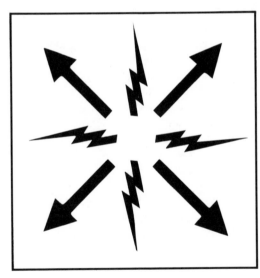

The case studies in this section relate to the complexities of curriculum implementation. At issue are questions regarding provision of released-time for in-service education, the fit between curriculum and evaluation, effects of published programs on curriculum decisions, and incorporating cognitive education into the curriculum. As a curriculum administrator, what should be your priorities in these and similar areas of implementation?

Case Study 6

Developing Professional Enthusiasm

Issue: Inservice time for experienced teachers

By the end of her first full year as director of curriculum in the Little Creek School District, Jane Hamilton had finished assessing the district's teachers for their awareness of current trends in education. She had also initiated curriculum improvement committees in three subject areas: mathematics, science, and English. These three committees were charged with completing a first draft of a revised curriculum within 12 months and recommending plans for implementing the changes through some form of inservice education. However, Hamilton's assessment of teacher awareness indicated an immediate need for a series of workshops to improve teachers' background on changes that had occurred in the methods of teaching science, mathematics, and English in the past 10 years.

The majority of Little Creek's teachers were tenured and had been in the district for at least 12 years. They enjoyed a positive relationship with the parents in the community, who regarded them with respect.

Yet it was clear to Hamilton that the science teachers were not involving students in active discovery experiences. The mathematics teachers, while knowledgeable about their subject, were following a didactic approach with relatively few visual aids or concrete experiences for students. And the English teachers as a group tended to use the same works of literature from year to year and to require only minimal writing from students.

Thus, Hamilton prepared a report, phrased in highly positive terms, listing the methodologies that would improve each subject-area program. She mentioned that she had located some talented master teachers in neighboring districts who could provide workshops on these new methodologies and a professor at the nearby teacher training institution who could provide leadership and cohesion to a series of workshops.

Understanding that a respected and dedicated corps of teachers who already enjoyed a positive reputation would need some incentive for participating in a workshop series, Hamilton also recommended that half-day released-time workshops be provided once a week for 10 weeks each semester. She discussed the idea with the officers of the Teachers' Association, who gave it their full support, and then with the superintendent, who, while also supporting it, realized that the community might be reluctant to accept the concept of released time for teachers since this was the first time it had ever been proposed.

The superintendent agreed to place the item on the agenda of the school board meeting, first as an information item and two weeks later as an action item. This would give the board and community members adequate time to discuss the issue. At the initial presentation of the report, the board supported the idea of helping experienced teachers become "up to date" by bringing specialized training into the district. However, two board members spoke out stridently against released time, stating that "teachers belong in the classroom, and children belong with them." At this point, the school board meeting was opened to the audience for questions.

The president of the Teachers' Association underlined the importance of recognizing professionalism by giving time for teachers to have additional training. The president of the Parent-Teachers Association then spoke against the notion of released time because parents expect teachers to engage in self-improvement on their own time after the regular school day. Another parent described the serious inconvenience to working parents if the children were to be dismissed from school early one day each week. The board then invited interested members of the professional staff and the community to make their ideas known to the superintendent and school board before the next meeting, when a decision would be reached.

The next day, the superintendent conferred with Hamilton to learn if there were any possible alternative to released time. The curriculum director considered carefully before replying because she perceived that the decision on this matter would be pivotal in determining whether or not there could be significant change in the professional staff in the foreseeable future.

Discussion Questions

1. Several alternatives were open to the director of curriculum in replying to the superintendent's request. They include providing after-school workshops on a voluntary basis, paying teachers for going to such workshops and making their attendance mandatory, reducing the number of released-time sessions per year, staying with the original recommendation because it is based on a careful assessment, and more. Select one of these alternatives or any other you can think of and defend it so as to convince the superintendent to bring it before the school board.

2. At the next school board meeting, what rationale should the superintendent present when he turns to the curriculum director for a revised recommendation?

3. Before the next school board meeting, what kind of conversations should occur between the Teachers' Association officers, school principals, and the trusted members of the professional staff, whom the curriculum director regards as potential leaders in effecting curriculum change in the district?

Case Study 7

Assessing Curriculum Change

Issue: Fit between evaluation techniques and outcomes

The Science Curriculum Committee of the Wakefield School District spent two years developing a revised and expanded science curriculum for the elementary grades. This effort involved a professor of science education from a nearby university as an outside consultant, a group of the district's teachers who investigated a variety of new materials and methods, and two science specialists from the high school level who provided the committee with information on the current content of science.

The written curriculum guide for elementary science included a list of specific objectives and a careful description of methods for actively engaging students in individual and small-group science investigations. The curriculum committee also engaged the services of a science education expert from a nearby district to conduct teacher workshops in a series of five Wednesday afternoon meetings. At those meetings, all of the teachers had opportunities to talk about the science content of the new curriculum and to carry out a series of hands-on investigations in physical sciences—an area the majority of elementary teachers had had difficulty with in the past. In addition, each of the elementary school principals attended at least one of the workshops so as to be better able to supervise teachers in the methodology, which involved considerable student activity.

The director of curriculum, Betty Warfield, met with the director of evaluation, whose role was to focus on assessment for the district as a whole, both individual and group. This meeting resulted in a written model for evaluating the new curriculum using as a baseline the science content portion of a well-known standardized achievement test. Because this test was given each spring at all grade levels, this year's test results would be used as the baseline measure for assessing any effects of the new science curriculum one year later.

At the completion of the workshop series at the end of October, teachers were told that they were fully qualified to implement the curriculum starting immediately. The teachers agreed to provide constructive feedback to Warfield, who would pass it to the curriculum committee for consideration for necessary revisions.

During the course of the academic year, the majority of the teachers taught the new curriculum on an average of twice a week. A few of the teachers were reluctant to give students as much self-directed activity as the curriculum called for, but they were encouraged by their principals to at least make the attempt. All but three of these teachers did so by working with a "partner" teacher and by combining classes to provide a mutual support system. Records of implementation indicated that most of the teachers had implemented the curriculum at least as frequently as the curriculum committee had recommended. Most of them were doing so by emphasizing student activity with investigations—a major departure from previous science teaching in the school district, which had emphasized *reading about and discussing* science topics *without manipulation.*

In the spring the director of evaluation administered the annual achievement test and worked closely with the test-correction service to pull out scores on the science subsection so that he could compare them with the previous year's scores. A statistical analysis of the difference between the mean scores of all elementary students in the district from the pretest with the means on the posttest (both districtwide and school by school) clearly indicated no statistically significant differences. The majority of the items on the achievement test were content items as opposed to process items. On the other hand, parents' unsolicited comments to school principals had indicated their enthusiasm about the new emphasis on children's active involvement in "sciencing." And teachers had reported to the science curriculum committee that they were more enthusiastic themselves because their students were looking forward to science periods.

The science curriculum committee had agreed earlier to provide the school board with the pretest and posttest data. The committee's chair prepared a summary report, which included the fact that the achievement test scores did not show statistically significant differences as a result of the new curriculum. But he added a paragraph describing the great enthusiasm for the new program on the part of parents and students as well as teachers.

When the report was received by the superintendent, he immediately challenged the committee to defend the worth of the new curriculum since it hadn't resulted in measurable improvements in test scores. He asked to meet with the committee, and the chair agreed.

At the meeting, the superintendent said, "I don't understand how you can say this new science curriculum is worth the time. There is absolutely no proof of its effectiveness in these evaluation results." One especially well-respected science teacher countered, "This year, for the first time ever, I heard my kids groan when science class was over and we had to finish up; surely, something positive is happening here even if the test scores don't show it." Another teacher added, "This is the first time in my 21 years of teaching that I've heard actual conversation about the science curriculum among teachers over coffee break in the teachers' room—these teachers are now involved."

After more exchanges, the superintendent ended the meeting by saying, "Okay, if both teachers and students are so involved and enthusiastic, I want you to find some way to produce measurable results in the coming year; if not, I will have to ask that we use the previous curriculum in our district again; give me some proof!" On the way out, the chair of the science curriculum committee commented to one of the teachers, "I know that at least two members of the school board feel the same as the superintendent, and they can really influence his thinking. We'd better do some 'selling' here."

The next day the science curriculum chair met with the director of curriculum to report the superintendent's ultimatum. He asked the director, "Can you give us a sense of direction for the coming year so that we can give the superintendent what he wants?"

Discussion Questions

1. What are the most important issues in this case for the teachers? The superintendent? The director of curriculum? The students?

2. What plan is feasible for the science committee and the school district to follow for the coming year, in response to the superintendent's ultimatum?

3. What evaluation techniques would give the superintendent evidence of the changes that were taking place in *children* as a result of the new curriculum?

4. Describe at least one positive and one negative aspect of using standardized achievement tests as a criterion measure for assessing the effects of a new curriculum.

Case Study 8

Curriculum Materials: Which Criteria to Use

Issue: Effect of published programs on local curriculum decisions

Washington High School served 1,500 students from a range of socioeconomic backgrounds. Before accepting his appointment, the new principal, Steven Wong, told the superintendent that one of his priorities would be to make sure the school's curriculum was up to date. He said he was particularly aware that changes in the mathematics field in the past five years were not reflected in the school's curriculum.

During the second week of the school year, Wong met with the chair of the department of mathematics, Mary Morello. They discussed the importance of keeping a curriculum up to date and agreed that curriculum revision should be a priority for the year. Morello pointed out that the textbook used in the mathematics department for algebra was out of date and should be replaced. Wong agreed that current materials were also important. They decided that Morello would form a committee of teachers to revise the curriculum and select a new text for algebra by March.

At its first meeting, the committee, composed of five faculty members and chaired by Morello, discussed the problems of the current mathematics program. One of the department members said, "I think one of the basic problems we have is that the algebra text is out of date, and I would like to work with someone else to find a good new one right away." Morello enthusiastically accepted this volunteer and appointed another teacher to work with her. Two other department members agreed that a new text in geometry should also be found and volunteered to begin that search. Morello agreed to have a school secretary contact the major publishers for samples of their most current texts in both fields and to have them available for analysis for the next four weeks.

Within two weeks, eight publishers provided copies of their high school texts for both algebra and geometry. The two subcommittees eagerly examined and compared the books and began to narrow down the possible choices. One day, Principal Wong ran into Mary Morello in the cafeteria and asked, "How is the curriculum committee doing?" "Just fine," Morello replied. "We have two subcommittees who volunteered to examine the new texts that are available in algebra and geometry, and they should be making recommendations to us soon so that we can go ahead with the work of the committee." Wong expressed satisfaction and wished the committee good luck.

When the math curriculum committee reconvened six weeks later, Morello asked for their reports and recommendations. The algebra subcommittee had brought two texts to the meeting. "We looked at more than half a dozen possibilities for the algebra text and narrowed the choice down to these two. Then we ran into difficulty. Both of these have up-to-date information, and the reading level seems to be about in the middle range for our students. But we finally chose this one by Jones and Petrie because the quality of the binding is better—these will last longer than the other one. So, we want to recommend Jones and Petrie for adoption." After a brief discussion, the consensus was to accept the recommendation of the algebra subcommittee.

Morello then turned to the other subcommittee. "What is your decision on the geometry text?" The subcommittee replied that they, too, reviewed all of the submitted texts and found it easy to eliminate all except two possibilities. "Then we took a hard look the remaining two and decided to recommend this one by Brown and Washington. Both of these choices are pretty current and the bindings seem to be of the same quality, but this one by Brown and Washington has the edge on graphics—they're more glossier and represent geometric figures better." Again, the rest of the math committee agreed to support the recommendation and to send both recommendations to the school principal.

Morello then declared that the committee's next task was to revise the school's mathematics curriculum guide. She asked that the format include a set of objectives for each of the courses in the curriculum, a list of the content topics for each course (in sequence), a list of tests that would be used for each course if commercially published tests were to be purchased, and the name or names of the texts for each course. The subcommittees that had been working on the selection of the algebra and geometry texts suggested that the algebra and geometry courses should logically be revised first. Morello agreed.

The committee met again two weeks later, and Morello asked for draft copies of the algebra and geometry courses. In each case, the set of objectives closely matched those in the newly adopted texts, the sequenced list of content topics reflected the general sequence in the table of contents of the new texts, and the recommended tests to be used at the end of each course were those published by the publisher of the new texts. The subcommittees reported that their curriculum guides would allow an excellent fit between what the school must do and what the materials would provide. Morello remarked that since it was already January, it would be important to move forward quickly with the revision of the school curriculum in the other fields—trigonometry, calculus, and general mathematics. The committee members agreed to consult with the teachers of those subjects and to collect their ideas and change the existing curriculum guides for those courses. The committee set a date to meet again three weeks later.

At that meeting the members reported that they had met with the instructors for the courses in trigonometry, calculus, and general math. In each case, the instructors expressed satisfaction with the current text and provided editorial changes for the existing curriculum guide. Morello asked for the edited drafts and noted that all three topic areas included a change in the date to the most recent edition of the texts, the addition of an objective on computer literacy or computer applications, and in trigonometry the change in the name of the test to be used at the end of the course to a new title published by the publisher of the course text. The chairman expressed appreciation to the committee members for their efforts and agreed to have the work retyped along with the curriculum guides for algebra and geometry, and to submit the package to the school principal by the end of February, well within the deadline.

For the concluding meeting with the math department chair, Wong had in front of him a copy of the school's existing curriculum guide in mathematics as well as the freshly typed revised curriculum. He asked Mary Morello to summarize the work of the committee and its recommendations for changes. Morello described the process that was used, indicated there would be recommendations for two different texts for the coming year, and showed Wong the five sections of the curriculum guide that corresponded to the five math topic areas. Wong then compared the "old" and "new" curriculum guides and asked Morello to indicate where changes were made since the guides seemed to be similar in several respects. Morello indicated that the sequence and content of the topics in algebra and geometry were the most different, and that the rest were minor revisions. When Wong asked what criteria were used for deciding on the new texts, Morello listed reading level, quality of binding, quality of graphics, and "up-to-dateness." The principal expressed his appreciation for that more detailed explanation.

Discussion Questions

1. If you were the school principal in this meeting, what responses would you make to this report from the math curriculum committee in terms of its completeness and acceptability for the task that was originally assigned?

2. In what ways did the committee's work qualify as curriculum revision, and in what ways did it not?

3. Critique the criteria used by the committee in analyzing and selecting the new texts.

4. What criteria would you recommend that the committee use in selecting texts for each course?

5. If you were the school principal, how would you have provided a different or more detailed charge to the math committee?

6. If you were the department chair in mathematics, what changes would you have made in the sequence of activities followed by the curriculum committee?

7. Describe in detail the most appropriate relationship between text selection and the development of a curriculum for the school in that subject.

Case Study 9

Finding "Room" for Thinking Skills

Issue: Incorporating cognitive education into the curriculum

Hawley Hills was a small city with light industry centered around several new electronics companies, but with a segment of the population still working for a silver mine that had been operating since 1873. The city also had a segment of younger, college-educated adults and another group of older residents whose education had ended with high school. The Hawley Hills Schools enjoyed a reputation of being focused on a coordinated and no-nonsense K-12 curriculum.

A year earlier, the director of instruction had arranged for a curriculum consultant to present an overview to all middle school teachers on a new program for teaching thinking skills. The workshop, held on a regularly scheduled staff development day, produced an enthusiastic response from the teachers in the two middle schools. As a result, 25 teachers of English, mathematics, and social studies made a commitment for in-depth staff training in how to teach specific cognitive skills within the regular curriculum.

Just before the next school year started, these 25 teachers participated in a two-and-a-half-day workshop on methods and materials for the teaching of thinking skills across all subject areas. As a part of their training, the teachers practiced some cognitive activities on an adult level and prepared model lesson plans for including thinking skills into their regular classes. Each one also had a chance to teach one model lesson to the rest of the teacher group. At the end of the workshop, the leader asked the teachers to say a few words about their plans for implementation. Each participant presented a plan for including the teaching of thinking skills at least twice a week in the regular curriculum. Several teachers expressed enthusiasm. Said one, "I've been so frustrated in teaching when I ask students to think through a problem and they just give me the first answer that pops into their heads; I think that *this* program will really help them to think through with better reasoning."

The first follow-up workshop was scheduled for October 30, during another staff workday, and the same workshop leader returned with additional materials and techniques to share. On the morning of the workshop, the leader began by asking participants to say a few words about how the new thinking skills program was proceeding in their classrooms.

A math teacher was the first to respond: "When I left our workshop at the end of August, I was enthusiastic, but when I presented some of these thinking skills activities to my students, they really turned off because they couldn't see what connection this has with math. I kept trying, by being enthusiastic and saying things like, 'Today I have a great way for you to learn how to think better,' but that still didn't work. So I haven't done very much since the second week of school."

A social studies teacher admitted, "I've had some of the same problems, although I was terribly pleased when I saw some of my children who hadn't had much success before suddenly succeed with activities that require some thinking. Still, this new program means I teach less of the subject-matter facts. It's slowing me down; I'm not as far along in our curriculum as I usually am at this time of year."

An English teacher added, "I still think it's fine for us to be emphasizing some things through this program—like analyzing, synthesizing, classifying, planning, and so on. Although I don't cover as much content, I've continued with the program because my students are more responsible and independent in getting the facts on their own. But I sure am getting some strange looks from my department chair when she comes in to observe—I've had to repeatedly assure her that we'll complete the literature book by the end of the year. My students are taking more responsibility for understanding the literature I'm teaching, and I think they'll be better prepared for next year's teachers. But she seems very concerned about that, and I'm starting to get some flack from some of my friends in the department who will have these kids next year."

Another participant from the math department caused heads to nod in agreement when she said, "I guess I'm going through that, too, even though I'm in a different department. I still think those skills are good for kids, but I also think we'll pay a price. The district achievement tests that we have to give in May won't show anything from our spending this much time on thinking skills; the multiple-choice tests don't look at this kind of skill. I think I may have really put myself out on a limb by joining this group."

The curriculum director looked anxiously at the workshop leader for her response to these rather disturbing comments. She stated, "I was going to give the rest of the group a chance to add to your comments, but I can see that we have a pattern of concerns emerging here, and I think we should address them before going on with the next level in our training." She turned to the curriculum director and said, "We've heard a number of problems and concerns from this fine group of teachers. Some of them have to do with finding the appropriate way of including thinking skills in the curriculum; others are about whether or not thinking skills even have a place in the curriculum here in Hawley Hills. Let's take a short coffee break and then take a good look at the ideas that have been raised."

The teachers went out to get coffee, and the workshop leader and the curriculum director moved to one side to discuss how to respond and to find some way of keeping the thinking skills plans for the district "on track" for this year.

Discussion Questions

1. The workshop leader had originally planned to spend the rest of the workshop day focusing on new materials for teaching thinking at still higher levels. In what ways should she change this plan?

2. How should the curriculum director address the concern about "covering the textbook" for this year in response to pressure from "next year's" teachers?

3. How can teachers address student concerns about the relevance of thinking skills to their learning in the subject?

4. The concern about student achievement on the May achievement tests was deep; how should the curriculum director and workshop leader deal with that concern at the workshop? For the rest of the

year? What implications would this concern have for district evaluation policy?

5. What long-range plans for curriculum revision may be appropriate for the inclusion of thinking skills as a regular part of the district curriculum?

6. What is your position on the ways in which cognitive skills have or do not have a justifiable place in the curriculum?

7. When teachers explicitly focus on thinking skills and students rebel by saying they want to learn only the subject at hand and don't see the relevance, how should teachers change the way they present cognitive skills activities?

Group III. Cases in Personnel and Curriculum

The next six cases involve the interaction of curriculum with personnel issues such as philosophical conflict among teachers, possible conflict of interest for school employees who "moonlight," a teacher work slowdown, and teacher ethics. All are multifaceted situations that raise many questions regarding the role of a curriculum director. Where would you stand if you were the director of curriculum faced with these situations?

Case Study 10

Conflict of Interest

Issue: The line between proper service to children and "moonlighting" by professionals

Jim Moore was a highly dedicated and experienced teacher of mentally handicapped children in the Turtle Tree School District. For eight years he had successfully taught a self-contained class of 15 children, with one instructional aide. The children worked with academic materials up to the limits of their potential and were provided many experiences outside the school to enrich their education. Several times a week they interacted with children in regular classes in music, art, and physical education, as well as in special school events. Over the years, Mr. Moore's students had made great strides; a few of them had even managed to return to regular classes.

Mr. Moore's reputation was so positive that parents of mentally handicapped children outside the district had been known to move to Turtle Tree just so their children could participate in his class.

To supplement his income, Jim Moore also worked every afternoon and evening as coordinator of the private, for-profit Learning Clinic, which was located in a nearby community outside the Turtle Tree School District. The child clients of the clinic were given remedial education in a variety of subject areas, at the request of parents and sometimes sending school districts. *Some* of the children came from Turtle Tree as well.

In the Turtle Tree School District, Individual Educational Plans (IEPs) for the following academic year were developed during April and May. Teachers of children with special needs were expected to work with the parents to develop each child's IEP, prepare a draft, and bring it to a meeting of the district's IEP committee. At that meeting, the curriculum director and others connected with special education discussed the IEP arrangements with the child's parents. As required by law, if the committee and parents failed to agree on the IEP, an appeals process would be initiated.

Thus, Mr. Moore developed the IEPs for his 15 students, all of whom would remain in his classroom next year. With his experience and knowledge, Moore was well aware of possible additional services each child might need—in some cases psychological services, in other cases medical assistance, and in still other cases additional academic assistance beyond the school day. Of his 15 children, he recommended that five receive additional academic assistance during afternoons, evenings, or weekends.

He recommended sending two of the five children to the Learning Clinic, which could provide the most appropriate service, given these children's need for perceptual activities relating to learning disabilities that compounded their mental handicapping conditions.

Mr. Moore understood the potential problems posed by this recommendation since, in a sense, he would indirectly profit from it (although he was *salaried* by the clinic). He met with the parents of those two particular children and explained this problem as well as the benefits the clinic could provide and the fit between the children's needs and the clinic's services. Both parents accepted the recommendation and seemed unconcerned about any potential conflict of interest.

Moore then sent the IEPs to the director of curriculum, Dee Dee May (who also served as the director of special education) for review prior to the joint meeting between the parents and other specialists. Normal procedure required the presence of the child's teacher as well as the signature of the teacher, along with that of the parent and other administrators, on any agreed-upon IEP.

May, after reading Mr. Moore's recommendation, asked to visit the Learning Clinic. Moore enthusiastically welcomed the curriculum director, who visited during an afternoon session and observed that the clinic's diagnostic and prescriptive activities were sound. However, another independent clinic located in a nearby town was also able to provide the services Moore's students needed. Curriculum Director May visited that clinic, too, and was equally satisfied with its credentials and procedures.

Noting the potential problem, May discussed the situation with a special education expert at the office of the county superintendent of schools. His advice was to avoid any possible conflict of interest by recommending the other clinic on the IEP rather than the one at which Jim Moore worked.

Dee Dee May returned to her office to prepare for the upcoming IEP meeting. As she pondered the factors in the situation, Mr. Moore appeared at her door and asked, "Well, are you going to make me re-write those two IEPs?"

Discussion Questions

1. What factors favored permitting both children to attend the Learning Clinic for services?

2. What factors, both immediate and future, would support writing into the IEPs a *different* educational clinic?

3. How would you reply to Moore's question?

4. If the curriculum director were to recommend keeping the IEPs as written, how should she respond if one of the parents or the county officer challenged the potential conflict of interest?

5. What policy changes in the school district would you institute in order to prevent problems like this from occurring in the future?

Case Study 11

Teacher Work Stoppage

Issue: Loyalty to teachers vs. administration

Hollis Montgomery, superintendent of the Clinton School District, had called a meeting of the nine principals of the district's schools, the business manager, and Sarah Feinstein, director of curriclum.

"As you know," he began, "the school board has been resisting the Teachers Association's request to grant a 6 percent salary increase to teachers this year. The board feels that 4 percent is adequate, given our dwindling resources and the fact that teachers still want to work here because we offer relatively desirable working conditions. The Teachers Association, on the other hand, has been adamant. Considering its new leadership and the fact that the school board also has some pretty strong-minded members, I don't think we'll have an accommodation by either side this time.

"In fact, about a half hour ago, I was informed that, starting tomorrow, unless there's significant progress in the salary discussions, the Teachers Association will ask all members to arrive at school at the latest possible time before classes start and leave immediately after classes end. They'll be involved solely in teaching and won't do any other kind of work." Montgomery looked around the table at each staff member and concluded, "We need to be ready for the next step after that; it may be a strike."

After considerable discussion, the group came up with a plan: Administrators would be expected to keep the schools operating by teaching combined classes wherever possible, supplemented by substitute teachers. Montgomery's secretarial staff was already calling a corps of substitute teachers in case a strike occured within a few days.

The next day, all but a few teachers arrived at school two

minutes before the first class and left right after the final bell. This forced Curriculum Director Feinstein to cancel an important meeting with Roger Chernault, chair of the social studies curriculum development committee. Chernault stopped by Feinstein's office for a moment to explain why, although he felt strongly about the importance of the current curriculum revision effort, he needed to maintain his loyalty to the Teachers Association. He believed all the teachers had to stay together on this issue. Feinstein acknowledged his concern: "I understand the situation you're in, and I appreciate your taking the time to stop by and explain it—I hope this thing can get finished quickly so that we can go back to what we must get done with our district programs."

Meanwhile, the school board issued a statement reiterating its firm offer of a 4 percent salary increase for teachers. Two more days passed. Finally, the president of the Teachers Association announced that, effective the following morning, teachers would suspend their duties until the situation was resolved. The contingency plan then flowed into action—substitute teachers were hired, and school administrators met to decide which classes required coverage and which ones could be combined. With the help of substitutes, parent volunteers, and administrators, the district managed to keep the schools open. With administrators working in the classrooms, only a minimal amount of time was devoted to administrative functions.

Curriculum Director Feinstein was paired with the junior high school principal to cover nine social studies classes each day. One of them was a class normally taught by Roger Chernault, the chair of the social studies curriculum committee. Feinstein felt a mixture of anxiety and anticipation as she took her post in front of that class for the first time. Adding to the excitement was a group of teachers marching right outside the classroom window, carrying signs urging the school board to be reasonable. A former social studies teacher herself, Feinstein decided that this would be an excellent opportunity to discuss the social issues in the community that influenced situations of this sort. As the students enthusiasticly discussed the topic, Feinstein noticed Chernault stop at the window and look in. Fortunately, the students' backs were to the window, so none of them saw his angry stare when he realized what was happening in the classroom. Feinstein ignored him and continued with the lesson. She discovered that Chernault had promoted the Teachers Association's point of view on the work stoppage at considerable length in the past two weeks. The students expressed a clear bias against all forms of management, including school boards. As a representative of the administration, Feinstein felt an obligation to explain to the students the opposing point of view, but she was careful not to advocate it. An interesting debate followed, in which the students took roles at a mock school board meeting.

Feinstein's enjoyment of this experience was tempered by grave concern about her future relationship with Roger Chernault, on whom she had come to depend in his work with the curriculum committee. He also had an important rapport with other teachers, and it was because of his reputation among the teachers that there had been such a high level of involvement and interest by the social studies teachers in the new curriculum changes.

Immediately after school, Feinstein visited Superintendent Montgomery, who asked, "How did it go today, Sarah?" She replied, "I had a great time, but I think I've probably paid a tremendous price in terms of our curriculum efforts in the district." She explained Chernault's disturbance about her coverage of his classes and read aloud a note she had just received from him:

Sarah—

When I saw you teaching my class today, I was struck by the fact
that our relationship has changed. I understand that you had to act
as an administrator, but I think there are some far more important principles involved here than covering classes. I thought we had
established a relationship that was based on cooperation between administration and teachers for the first time; I think we've lost
that now, and I, for one, am sorry for you.

Roger

Montgomery considered for a moment and then said, "Sarah, I know you've worked hard to establish an excellent working relationship with the teachers, and the curriculum results show it. The school board is also very pleased with what they see as the first steps toward real coordination among teachers that has happened in recent years. Right now we're in a bind; the issue concerns not only the fiscal health of the district, but the appropriate distribution of power between the school board and the teachers. The board *must* make this kind of decision."

Feinstein made no response, and Montgomery continued, "However, it seems to me that we probably have enough coverage for classes for the next several days. If you feel that any further participation as a representative of the administration will place you in an impossible position with the curriculum development processes, I can release you from covering any more classes. On the other hand, you need to remember that all of the other administrators, including school principals with whom you are also working, are covering classes. Still, I think your position is very sensitive and certainly different from mine or that of a site administrator. So I'll leave the decision up to you. Would you let me know before you go home today what you want to do?"

Sarah returned to her own office to weigh the situation on all sides; she had only two hours to make a decision.

Discussion Questions

1. To what extent was Sarah Feinstein's involvement in covering classes during a work stoppage a short-term threat to her further work with curriculum committees of teachers? To what extent was it a long-term threat?

2. In what ways would she affect her relationship with other school administrators if she decided not to participate in administrative coverage of classes?

3. If you were Feinstein, in what ways would you attempt to reestablish your relationship with Chernault at this point? At the end of the work stoppage?

4. What decision would you make if you were Feinstein in this case? Why?

Case Study 12

Textbook Selection Policies and Procedures

Issue: Teacher ethics and board ethics

The tension in the administrative offices of the Alta Vista School District was mounting. The school board meeting scheduled for that night was sure to be a hot one. A few months earlier, the task of selecting new high school French books had seemed to be a straightforward matter. Somehow, it had turned in a major school-community issue. Newspaper reporters, parents, and teachers throughout the district—an ethnicaly mixed, central California community of 35,000—were discussing the issue, taking sides, and "fanning the flames into a major fire."

Several months earlier, Jean Bentz, director of curriculum and instruction, had convened a committee of nine foreign language teachers from the four secondary schools to begin the process of selecting new French books. The district policy at that time mandated that new textbooks were to be approved by all the schools at the grade level under discussion.

The first meetings of the committee started out rather quietly, with the group going through the usual steps of discussing philosophy and methods, articulating the curriculum, and reviewing the proposed textbooks. After a great deal of deliberation and numerous meetings over a ten-week period, the teachers on the committee were still unable to agree on a book. Any proposed textbook would not affect Adams High School for at least five years since it had bought additional copies of the old title the year before. Bentz thus recommended to the superintendent that the selection preferred by Brigham High School be approved since that school needed new books quickly in order to have them by the September school opening.

Bentz made the first presentation to the school board in early July. To her astonishment, the board rejected her recommendation on the grounds that they had been told by "someone" that the proposed new book was "inferior" to the one presently used. Several board members had been receiving information privately from two faculty members at Adams High School.

The next day, Bentz reconvened the nine teachers to try once again to reach consensus on a new book that both schools would endorse. The second book was selected again primarily by the staff of Brigham High School. This new choice was endorsed by several independent foreign language experts in the region, as well as by the entire foreign language department from Adams High School, with the exception of one teacher. The teachers felt this new choice was a better book and all agreed to support its recommendation. The one dissenter was Bill Jones, who felt that the second book was no better than the first. He again expressed his views to three members of the school board who had been encouraging Jones to communicate directly with them.

Although the majority of the foreign language department of Adams High School felt that this second choice was superior to the first one, they decided to continue using their present book since they had many copies on hand. Curriculum Director Bentz said that would be acceptable and shouldn't cause any problems.

Bentz went back to the board to present the newest recommendation. Once again, the board rejected it and asked for a report *directly* from the two high school foreign language department chairpersons.

It was the end of July when Bentz called the nine teachers together once again to ask them to implement the board's request—to prepare their own presentations for a third board meeting regarding the French textbook. Many of the teachers from all four secondary schools were present at that final group meeting, including Bill Jones. They all discussed the issue again and *everyone*, including Jones, supported the recommendation that Bentz had first presented to the board. Since Jones had been so adamant about the "inferior" quality of the book, Bentz directly asked him if he would now support the recommendation so that the matter could be resolved. He replied that he would support the recommendation of all the teachers.

With agreement reached, the two department chairs prepared their presentations for the next board meeting. In the meantime, Jones wrote a letter to the board repeating his opinion about the inferior quality of the book that was about to be recommended by his colleagues.

Learning of Bill Jones' letter, Jean Bentz decided to write him a formal letter of reprimand, which would be placed in his personnel file. That letter caused another major issue to erupt when two board members accused Bentz of denying Jones his "freedom of speech."

The case then became a twofold issue concerning (1) the adoption of a textbook and (2) the curriculum director's "right" to reprimand a teacher by placing a letter in the teacher's personnel file. Both issues continued to be front-page news in the local newspaper for several months.

Discussion Questions

1. What are the fundamental issues in this case?

2. What is your interpretation of this textbook controversy as a whole? What can you say about the board's role? Jones' role? Bentz's role?

3. What do you think of Jean Bentz's decision to place a letter in the teacher's personnel file?

4. How else might Bentz have handled the problem at the time of the first board denial?

5. If you had been the superintendent, what might you have said to the board prior to its second meeting on the choice of text?

Case Study 13

Teacher Curricular Autonomy

Issue: Resolving teacher conflict

Newborough School District served a once-rural community that had lately found itself in the throes of high technology development. The schools, which had been bastions of conservative educational ideology and practice, suffered their own upheaval. Enrollments were increasing, buildings were crowded, and teachers were feeling increased frustration. There were six elementary schools serving an average of 700 K-6 students each. The two junior high schools each had about 850 students in grades 7-9, and the high school enrolled about 1,500 grade 10-12 students. Class size was about 27 throughout the district, with elementary classes slightly smaller.

The newly apppointed superintendent arrived a year ago with her own agenda for change. One of her major concerns was to improve district curriculum coordination. Her predecessor had let each school manage its own curriculum, and principals in turn had given teachers a great deal of autonomy.

One of the superintendent's first moves was to appoint K-12 curriculum coordinators for all the major subject areas. In each case she selected an *outsider*, even though several of the local teachers had applied for the positions. The new reading/language arts coordinator was Penny McArthur. McArthur held very forward-looking views about reading and language arts; she actively espoused a "whole-language" approach that emphasized students' active use of language and minimized the teaching of formal grammar and "fragmented" reading skills.

At McArthur's recommendation, the superintendent also appointed a committee to revise the English/language arts curriculum for the entire district. The committee included two elementary teachers, two junior high teachers, two high school teachers, and the junior high principal. (One of the high school teachers, Mike Davis, had applied for the coordinator's position.)

At the first meeting of the committee in April, McArthur began by explaining the committee's charge and assuring members that she believed in participatory decision making. She noted that she wanted to develop a "consensus curriculum" that teachers would support and implement. However, she also stressed the need for a quality curriculum that would reflect the best current theory and research on language development.

She then suggested that the committee members briefly describe their individual perceptions of the present curriculum. One of the elementary teachers said she thought the curriculum was "quite good now" and wasn't sure why any revision was necessary. She added, "I think there are more important problems to solve—like reducing class size." One of the junior high teachers said he saw a need for a coordinated grammar curriculum. His students were bored with grammar; they told him that they had been studying grammar since 3rd grade. He thought the study of grammar should begin in grade 6 and end by grade 9, with high school teachers doing a review as necessary. Mike Davis then made a long speech about how inadequately the students were prepared in grammar. He said, "They come to me without knowing what a subject is, and I have to spend my time patching up their knowledge. I'm not blaming anybody—I just think we have to get the problem straightened out."

Somewhat impatiently, McArthur interjected her own views. She cited the many research studies indicating that the study of formal grammar did not improve students' ability to speak, write, or read— and, in fact, took away valuable time from other more important content. She then referred to the research on children's cognitive development, which in her view proved that students did not have sufficient cognitive maturity to understand abstract concepts until at least grade 9. She thought the best answer was to use a whole-language approach from kindergarten to grade 8 and then teach a course in linguistics in high school.

For a few minutes there was an awkward silence. Finally, one of the elementary teachers spoke out in a sullen and defensive manner. Her 4th grade pupils had no trouble understanding grammar, she said, because she used different learning modalities. And she knew that their writing was better than many because she showed them how to apply grammatical knowledge in writing better sentences.

Anyway, she pointed out, the district had just purchased a brand new elementary language arts textbook series that included formal grammar. The other elementary teacher strongly supported her, noting that she knew teachers in all the elementary schools and they all believed that grammar was important.

Davis now joined in. He observed that a neighboring district had once tried a linguistics approach and had abandoned it because it was too difficult for students. "We just don't have time at the high school to teach linguistics; I already have trouble *now* getting through two Shakespeare plays and four novels," he added.

The junior high principal tried to resolve the obvious conflict. "Look, let's do some problem solving. Why not survey all the language arts and English teachers and ask them what *they* think we should do about grammar? You know, if they want to teach grammar, they're going to do so anyway, regardless of what we say. They close the classroom door, and they *become* the curriculum. I don't see any sense in publishing some big fat curriculum guide that gets put on the shelf."

When Davis saw that McArthur did not seem happy with that suggestion, he saw a chance to score some points against her. "That's a great idea. That will help us carry out Penny's ideas about participatory decision making."

A new coordinator, McArthur was obviously discomfitted. She decided that her best strategy would be to buy some time. "Well, that's an idea to consider. But remember, we have the whole language arts curriculum to think about, not just grammar. And I don't think we can settle curriculum issues by taking a vote. But it's getting late. Let's adjourn now and think it over until our next meeting."

Discussion Questions

1. Describe what you believe should be the optimal solution in this struggle between what the teachers want the curriculum to be and what "experts" believe it should be.

2. Assume that the teachers on the committee accurately represented the views of the other English/language arts teachers in their schools. If you were Penny McArthur, what would be your long-term *strategy* in resolving this conflict and achieving the optimal solution you identified above?

3. What mistakes, if any, do you think McArthur made in the way she conducted this initial committee meeting?

4. McArthur's summary of the research on the teaching of formal grammar was accurate. Given this body of research, how do you explain the fact that the teaching of grammar has persisted so strongly?

5. In what ways do you believe that McArthur's summary of the research on children's cognitive development was accurate? To what extent do you think decisions about grade-level content placement should be influenced by such research?

Case Study 14

Staffing for Curriculum Leadership

Issue: Optimal staffing patterns

Franklin School District was in a suburb of a large midwestern city. Until this year, it had enjoyed reasonably good economic health, but three months ago the major employer, a large manufacturer of military equipment, announced the closing of its plant due to losses of government contracts. Although the city council appointed a committee to attract new industry to the area, the school board decided that it had to make major budget cuts. And the board made it clear to the superintendent that those cuts were not to increase class sizes.

The district included a high school, three middle schools, and six elementary schools. The teachers, for the most part, had many years of experience in the district, and their principals generally considered them to be effective and competent in a rather conventional mode. In recent years, each elementary school had hired two new teachers; there were no plans to hire any additional teachers in the foreseeable future. All the teachers had recently participated in workshops on Elements of Effective Teaching, which the teachers considered useful but hadn't caused them to significantly change the way they taught.

The leadership picture at the building level was complex. The principals also were very experienced men and women; the superintendent believed that they were competent managers but not especially strong in curriculum and instruction. All the principals took an active interest in improving their teacher evaluation skills and believed they were doing a good job of supervising. They were required to observe each teacher three times each year; the superintendent required written reports to be sure they made the minimum number of visits.

The high school principal, who admitted that he was not strong in curriculum, had two assistants, one responsible for discipline and one for "curriculum and instruction." The assistant principal for curriculum and instruction was expected to devote half his time to what the principal vaguely referred to as "curriculum coordination" and the other half to supervision. In fact, the assistant spent all his time observing teachers and picking up the administrative "slack." He seemed unsure of the curricular aspects of his role and thus did no real curriculum work. The high school had eight department heads, who were given released time somewhat proportional to the size of their departments; heads of larger departments taught one or two classes instead of five; those of small departments taught four classes. The total released time for the department heads was the equivalent of three full-time teachers. The department heads did some classroom observation, none of it very effective. They seemed to spend most of their time orienting substitutes, managing instructional materials, holding meetings, and preparing for their own teaching.

In the middle schools, the principals considered themselves to be the curriculum leaders, although they actually spent very little time on curricular matters. Each had an assistant principal who handled all discipline and routine administrative matters. Each middle school also had three grade-level team leaders, who had one released period each day. The team leaders were expected to "coordinate the curriculum," although they spent little time on curricular issues. The one period of released time was usually spent in dealing with any crises and providing day-to-day support for team members. When the principals felt they needed some curricular expertise, they claimed they called on the district coordinators. However, these occasions were rare. Each middle school had one full-time reading specialist who worked chiefly with less able readers.

At the district level were two assistant superintendents, one of whom had the title "Assistant Superintendent for Curriculum and Instruction." The person holding this position devoted most of her time to arranging for staff development and supervising federal programs. There were seven "curriculum coordinators" for reading/language arts, social studies, mathematics, science, foreign language/bilingual education, fine and applied arts, and health and physical education. The coordinators were supposed to be primarily concerned with curriculum, although they also were expected to "improve instruction through supervision." Although the coordinators appeared to be busy, they were unproductive. They seemed unsure of their function and were chiefly *reactive*; they waited for their services to be requested. The exception was the mathematics coordinator, who took a very proactive role, especially at the elementary and middle school levels. She worked closely with teachers, developed instructional materials, held workshops, and did a great deal of classroom observation.

The curriculum varied in its quality. Once each year one of the major subjects was reviewed and revised; teacher committees worked during the summers to produce revised guides that varied in quality and impact. The elementary teachers generally used the guides, along with their textbooks, in deciding what to teach. The middle school and high school teachers, on the other hand, gave the guides a cursory examination and then put them aside. The mathematics guide was exemplary; the science guide was up to date even though it was textbook-driven; the other curriculum guides were marginal at best.

A consultant was called in to examine the situation. She first analyzed the present direct costs of curricular and supervisory services (exclusive of the assistant superintendent's salary). She then developed the following cost analysis:

1 high school assistant	$40,000
8 high school department heads, released time equivalent to 3 teachers @ $30,000	$90,000
3 middle school team leaders, released time equivalent to 3/5 teacher @ $30,000	$18,000
7 curriculum coordinators @ $40,000	$280,000
Total direct costs	$428,000

The consultant also interviewed and surveyed teachers. Her study yielded the following generalizations about teachers' perceptions:

1. The teachers tended to turn to their *colleagues* when they wanted help with curricular and instructional matters.
2. The high school teachers tended to support their department

heads but believed the heads had too much released time and spent too much time on "administrivia."
3. The middle school teachers voiced strong support for their team leaders.
4. The teachers—with the exception of the mathematics teachers—did not believe the district coordinators were of much help.
5. The teachers believed that major improvements were needed in all areas of the curriculum except mathematics.

The superintendent asked the consultant to recommend new staffing patterns in the area of curricular and supervisory leadership, with these guidelines:

1. The assistant superintendent for curriculum and instruction would remain in place, even though the nature of the role might be redefined.
2. Tenure would not be not an issue. Coordinators did not have tenure; school administrators could be reassigned.
3. The Teachers' Association contract was not a limiting factor. Positions could be reclassified and teachers reassigned.
4. The cost of direct curricular and supervisory services had to be reduced by approximately one-third, using the same salary figures.
5. Any new staffing patterns should reflect the best current knowledge relative to staffing for curricular and supervisory *leadership*.

Discussion Questions

1. What do you believe are the major weaknesses in the exising pattern?

2. If you were superintendent and budget cuts were not an issue, how would you upgrade the quality of the present leadership staff?

3. If you were the consultant, what staffing pattern would you recommend? In answering this question, please:
   a. Identify the role;

b. Briefly describe the scope of the role and the areas of responsibility;
c. Specify to whom this individual will report;
d. Indicate direct salary cost.

4. If your new staffing pattern were to be implemented, what major problems would you anticipate, and how would you deal with them?

Case Study 15

The Budget Squeeze

Issue: Defining "basics" vs. "frills"

Superintendents throughout the state of Minnesota were notified by the state superintendent of instruction that funding for schools would be reduced by 5 percent in the coming fiscal year. There was no prospect of budget relief from the legislature, and an additional local tax levy was unlikely. Upon hearing this news, the superintendent of the Larchmont School District made inquiries about all other avenues for funding.

It was clear that the Larchmont School District did indeed face a cut in its funding of both personnel and nonpersonnel items. Ninety-two percent of the district budget was personnel-related; any reduction of the other 8 percent devoted to nonpersonnel items would be impractical because of the basic supplies needed to operate the school system in the current year. Thus, some reduction in salaries was necessary. Because staff positions (as opposed to faculty) had been reduced in budget cuts two years ago, the district's only option at this point was to eliminate some faculty positions as well.

The final decision about what would be cut was required by March 31. During the preceding October, the superintendent of schools asked the director of curriculum, John Montesa, to establish and chair a 10-member districtwide committee composed of three parents and seven teachers to study the problem and make recommendations, prior to January 31, regarding program elimination or reduction.

The committee decided to separate into three subcommittees to study the respective curriculums at the elementary, middle school, and senior high levels. Each subcommittee had its own chair and agreed to present to the entire committee a recommendation for a cut that would be equivalent to at least 2 percent of the district budget. The parent members of the committee agreed to contact fellow parents in their neighborhoods, and the teacher members would consult with their colleagues back in the schools for ideas as well as feedback on the committee's progress.

The subcommittees deliberated and gathered data about the number of hours per week that students spent in each subject area. The parent members developed and sent a written survey to all parents in the school district, asking them to rank on a scale of one to five the importance of each subject area in the curriculum. After considerable telephone follow-up efforts by the parent members and another group of parents working with them, a 35 percent return from the survey was obtained across the district.

The teachers who polled their fellow teachers about ideas for this serious dilemma began at first to hear remarks that the district *could* make further cuts in *nonfaculty* areas, but they provided no suggestions for program cuts per se. After a week of deliberations by teacher members of the committee with fellow teachers, the president of the district Teachers' Association contacted Montesa to inform him of the Teachers' Association's official position: it would endorse *no* program cuts or faculty position cuts, and all members of the Teachers' Association (approximately 95 percent of the teachers in the district) were being instructed to avoid answering any questions about which programs should be eliminated or which positions should be cut.

The seven teacher members of the committee, however, agreed to continue serving as discussion participants at committee meetings, even though they would not make any recommendations because of their loyalty to the Teachers' Association. The initiative, then, for specific suggestions for action now fell to the parents and members of the community.

The committee decided to eliminate its subcommittee structure because of the stance of the Teachers' Association members and because the data from the parent survey appeared to provide ideas about all subject areas at all grade levels.

The tally of the survey results from individual families indicated that all parents put a high priority on the subject areas of reading, English, mathematics, social studies, science, and foreign languages, in that order. However, there was no perceptible difference in the rankings for those subject areas against each other. On the other hand, the rankings for physical education, music, home economics, health education, industrial arts, driver education, and art were all appreciably lower than those for the first goup of subject areas. (This result, of course, was consonant with the rankings of importance for subject areas in the general population.)

The committee scheduled a meeting to discuss this final tally. One of the parents made a presentation to the rest of the group: "These results clearly show that the parents are making a statement. No one is saying that art, music, physical education, or the often lower-ranked subjects are not important for children. But if we have to make some cuts, they have to be in those areas since we have a consensus that the other subjects are critical to keep." The other two parents supported this recommendation, but said they regretted eliminating or reducing any of the subject areas. Although the teacher members did not take a stand, one explained, "If we're serious about a balanced education for our children, then we should be making *no* cuts in programs."

The discussion continued in the same vein, and the parent members of the committee moved to send a report to the school board recommending the reduction or elimination of the programs in art, music, and physical education in order to achieve the necessary budget savings by reducing the faculty positions in those fields. The teacher members were unwilling to agree to this recommendation, and wanted to make a separate statement on the importance of keeping all aspects of the school program. The committee finally decided to make two reports representing both committee "factions."

John Montesa agreed to write a cover statement for this two-part report. The thrust of his statement was that all subject areas are important in a school curriculum, but when reductions are essential, they should not be in the major subject areas. And he suggested regionalizing the instruction in the reduced subject areas; that is, Larchmont and several neighboring districts could jointly support an itinerant specialist to provide instruction in each area.

Montesa submitted the report to the superintendent, who brought it to the school board for discussion. At the board's public meeting, the chair asked one parent member and one teacher member of the committee to explain the points of view of each subgroup. Montesa reiterated the position he made in the opening statement of the report, and then the chair of the board turned to the superintendent for a recommended action.

The superintendent replied, "This is very difficult, and I regret having to make this recommendation, but I believe we must reduce instruction in art and music as well as physical education, home economics, industrial arts, driver education, and health so as to maintain our strength in the other subject areas. I recommend that we give proper notice to the specialists in these areas so that they can seek employment elsewhere if they are not able to survive on a part-time salary." The school board then officially approved the recommendation and asked the superintendent to draw up an implementation schedule.

The implementation plan proposed that specialist teachers not be used to provide elementary students with art or music, but only to teach physical education once a week. In the middle school, the schedule for art, home economics, industrial arts, music, driver education, and physical education was reduced from two periods to one per week for each student, who would then be assigned an extra hour for library study.

At the senior high level, art, music, driver education, home economics, industrial arts, and physical education instruction would continue, as in the past, as elective courses only.

Discussion Questions

1. If you had been the curriculum director in this case, how would you have acted similarly or differently in working with the district-wide committee?

2. What alternatives would you have explored for making program cuts, if those cuts were indeed inevitable?

3. How would you have worked with the president of the Teachers' Association to ensure real participation by the teacher members of the study committee?

4. What criteria can you suggest that would help determine which elements of the curriculum are basic and which are nonessential?

5. What are your definitions of basic and nonessential curriculum subjects?

Group IV.
Cases in Programs
for Special
Populations

This section presents four cases on the relationship of district curriculum to special populations, such as students with limited-English proficiency or handicapping conditions. The issues include some of the current controversies in bilingual education, the role of principals in mainstreaming programs, the fears and demands of parents, the nature of curriculum in serving special populations, and the best use of restricted funds. Is there, or should there be, a process of defining curriculum for special-needs students? Is that curriculum a *piece* of the "regular education" curriculum, or is it separate but equal? As a curriculum administrator, how would you attempt to serve special populations?

Case Study 16

An Influx of Immigrants

Issue: How to best serve immigrant children

The Edwardville School District served students of families from a broad socioeconomic range and diverse ethnic backgrounds, and, until lately, most students were native speakers of English. The immigrant population was minimal.

Last year, Edwardville's City Council voted to permit a local real estate developer to build 500 units of low- and middle-income housing. When the units were finished a large number of Middle Eastern immigrants moved into them. The adults in those families, although unable to speak much English, valued education. Their children, especially those entering kindergarten and the lower elementary grades, seemed to learn English very quickly. On the other hand, the children starting in the upper elementary grades and beyond had more difficulty learning English (which is normal in the developmental cycle). Their teachers devoted a great deal of attention to ensuring that these children understood directions and were actively taught English vocabulary and grammar.

After two days of experience with this new student population, the teachers of upper elementary and secondary grades brought the situation to the attention of the principals. They, in turn, immediately discussed it with Superintendent Ron Willis and suggested providing special instruction in English-as-a-second-language (ESL). When Willis asked his director of curriculum to check into the guidelines, they quickly discovered that ESL instruction was both legally mandated and supported by funding for instructors.

Their subsequent search of the community and nearby universities identified several qualified ESL instructors, none of whom, however, was *bilingual* in English and any Middle Eastern language. Nevertheless, the district hired them on a part-time basis to work with the children in a daily "pull-out" ESL program. A month later, the regular classroom teachers reported noticeable improvement in the children's ability to function in the classroom.

Several weeks later, three parents of these children, along with an interpreter, visited Superintendent Willis to request that instruction not only be provided in English, but in the children's native language as well. Willis promised to take the request under consideration. He and the curriculum director decided to invite an expert in bilingual education to visit the school district and recommend how they should best proceed.

The consultant suggested that the district hire four special teachers to give these children instruction in their native language on a pull-out basis for at least one hour a day, in addition to the pull-out ESL program. When Willis reported this idea to the school board, they agreed to reallocate budget funds to pay for the additional instruction. Because it was difficult to find speakers of the Middle Eastern language who were also good teachers, a full month passed before the program could begin. Soon, however, all of the Middle Eastern children in grades 1 through 12 were receiving a daily hour of ESL instruction *and* an hour of instruction in their own language, some of which included such school subjects as mathematics.

Soon after this implementation, the Teachers Association held its annual all-member meeting and passed, by a large margin, a resolution that instruction in the Middle Eastern language be reduced or eliminated because it was "taking valuable time from regular instruction" and was not making the students "more fluent in English."

When this resolution appeared in the Edwardville newspaper, the local PTA board asked that the matter be discussed further at the administrative level. In the meantime, the board also drafted a resolution of its own supporting the teachers and emphasizing that the children needed to learn English to succeed in American society. This, the board averred, far exceeded the value of further instruction in the children's own language since they had already mastered it at home.

Superintendent Willis placed this item on the school board agenda and solicited a response from the representatives of the Middle Eastern parents group. The parents chose not to respond, but instead arranged for an attorney to attend the school board meeting to represent the right of their children to master their own language, under bilingual education laws.

Willis sent a formal request to the district's director of instruction to recommend to him, in writing, a course of action based on what would be best *educationally* for these children. Specifically, did the additional instruction in their native language sufficiently benefit the children to justify sacrificing time from the rest of the school day?

Discussion Questions

1. What are the fundamental political issues in this case?

2. What are the fundamental educational issues, aside from questions of law?

3. What is your position on bilingual education in which instruction is provided in the student's own language? Why?

4. If costs were not a consideration, how would you reply to the superintendent's question? How would you reply if costs were a major consideration?

5. How would you respond to the resolution by the Teachers Association?

6. How would you reply to the resolution passed by the Parent Teachers Association?

Case Study 17

Mainstreaming

Issue: Changes in methods and curriculum to make mainstreaming work

Filled with enthusiasm and optimism, Mrs. Gwendolyn Johnson, mother of nine-year-old Emily, sat down at the conference table, eager for the meeting about her child's Individualized Education Plan (IEP) to begin. Emily, with a moderate hearing impairment, was finally qualified to be placed in a regular classroom. Since the 2nd grade, Emily had been in a special day program for hearing-impaired children and had interacted with hearing children only on the playground and during some special school activities, such as art shows and the annual science fair. However, Emily's teacher and the school guidance counselor agreed that Emily's achievement in reading and other general academic progress had made it appropriate for her to join a regular classroom—that of Bill Schneider in the 4th grade.

Mrs. Johnson's enthusiasm came from her conversations with the mothers of other children in the class, and her joy that Emily would be with hearing children. Emily's speech patterns, while not completely normal, would probably not prevent her from having easy communication with hearing children in most situations. Instruction in the special day class for Emily had been in a combination of speaking and sign language (simultaneous communication), and Emily had spent considerable time each day on language development.

At the IEP meeting, guidance counselor Anne Parker announced, "After careful consideration, we are convinced that Emily is ready for a mainstream classroom, and that Mr. Schneider's classroom will be the best for her. His language program uses a small-group approach, and that will allow Emily to have the attention she needs."

Mrs. Johnson replied, "I'm very pleased that you feel Emily is ready for a mainstream classroom. I just have one question. Suppose Emily needs some further special instruction because of her deafness?" Parker responded, "We've already taken care of that.

Emily is going to have at least two half-hour appointments a week with the itinerant deaf-education specialist who comes to the school each Tuesday and Thursday."

They discussed timing, materials, and general logistics, and then Mrs. Johnson said, "Well, I'm ready to sign the appropriate papers." The meeting concluded after a flurry of signatures and exchanging of carbon copies.

Four weeks into the new school year, Mrs. Johnson called Anne Parker with several serious concerns and they arranged a meeting. The guidance counselor invited the director of special education, Al Rockwell, to sit in on the conference. Mrs. Johnson began. "I don't think this mainstream idea is going to work out. Emily comes home every night and cries for at least an hour; when I ask her what's wrong, she says she has no friends and she thinks she's falling behind in her work."

Parker asked for more elaboration. Mrs. Johnson explained that Emily was being avoided by other children on the playground because she "talks funny." Also, she saw her scores on Mr. Schneider's reading exercises and knew she had the lowest or the second lowest score on most activities in her group—the "low" group. Finally, Emily didn't understand some of what Mr. Schneider said to her because he didn't use sign language and his lips were hard to read.

The director of special education turned to Parker and asked, "On what basis was the recommendation for mainstreaming made?" Parker outlined the reasons that were given at the spring IEP meeting, and Rockwell nodded with understanding.

Mr. Schneider, who was waiting in a separate room, was invited to join the meeting. He offered his concern to the group. "Sometimes I think Emily gives up too easily, but I want you to know that I really want this to succeed." Rockwell asked Mr. Schneider some further questions about the classroom and the arrangement for Emily. Emily was receiving help in reading from the itinerant deaf-education teacher twice a week on a pull-out basis. But Parker added that she understood from the special teacher that much of those two periods was spent on "counseling" Emily on how to adjust to the classroom situation. Emily was very open about her concern that she didn't "fit in."

Rockwell asked Schneider about his background in special education. He replied, "Well, I had the required course for certification at the university in educating special populations, but I never took sign language because I didn't think I would ever need that. Also, because my class is smaller this year, I have no instructional aide, so I'm the only adult in the classroom and I have 24 other people besides Emily that I must work with."

Mrs. Johnson expressed her deep disappointment about the arrangement. "I had hoped that this experience would be the beginning of the chance for Emily to rejoin the rest of the world, since my husband and I truly want her to be able to identify with hearing children. She's worked only with other deaf children in the past three years. I do wish we could do something to make this succeed, but I'm afraid I may need to ask you to have her returned to the special day class."

The meeting concluded with the director of special education agreeing to call Mrs. Johnson after considering some alternatives for Emily.

Discussion Questions

1. The word "mainstream" never appears in the federal law relating to special education, although the legal term "least restrictive environment" does. What does that term really mean?

2. Under the circumstances in Emily's school, what is the most appropriate and least restrictive environment?

3. What additional information and preparation should the director of special education and the guidance counselor have made prior to the spring IEP meeting?

4. What specific arrangements would be necessary in order to make the regular classroom workable for Emily at this point? Be sure to focus on all relevant areas, such as teacher preparation, curriculum, and classroom assistance.

5. If appropriate arrangements could make the regular classroom workable for Emily, what steps would you, as the director of special education, take in relation to Emily's *feelings* about the situation? Could something be done to make her feel more positive, or is it too late for this year?

6. Develop a one-paragraph philosophy on mainstreaming that takes into account the conditions under which you believe it can be made to work well.

7. If you were the director of special education in a school district, what provisions would you make in the district's *written* curriculum to encompass the needs of mainstreamed students whose teachers have little background in special education?

Case Study 18

Concerns of Parents of Mainstreamed vs. Nonhandicapped Children

Issue: Developing reasonable IEPs for special-needs children and allaying parents' fears

For three years, two special education teachers in the Coolidge School District team-taught a class of 12 children identified as "educable mentally retarded." The children ranged in age from 7 through 11, and came from various areas within the district. The classroom was located in a separate building on the grounds of a large elementary school. The children in this class had virtually no interaction with the other children in the school; they ate their lunch separately and had separate exercise times on the playground and separate classes in their own building.

The school's new principal was Eleanor Eden. Although this special class was technically under the supervision of Tim Curtis, the district's director of special education, it was on the site of the elementary school, and Eden had some specific ideas about the class. After consulting with Curtis, who also served as the director of instruction for the district, Eden arranged with the two special education teachers to initiate some integration experiences for the children in the special class. These children would have a common play time with their age peers on the playground each morning and occasionally participate in special field trips with them. They would also eat lunch in the school dining hall with the rest of the students, although they could eat at their own table. Eden and the two teachers were also very enthusiastic about the idea of "reverse mainstreaming"; several children from the regular classes would spend time each day during science or art periods with the special-needs children in the special classroom, learning about science from the two team teachers and working with some of the special children.

Eden sent a letter to the parents of both the special-needs children and the children who would participate in the reverse mainstreaming activities. She explained that the new plan would benefit both groups of children.

Two days later Eden received a letter from a parent of one of the children in a regular classroom, with a copy sent to the director of special education, stating his grave concern that any regular interaction between his child and the special-needs children could well hold back his child's progress. The parent had written carefully but firmly and expressed his concern in terms of time taken away from challenging his child, who had been identified as "gifted and talented." No letters of concern appeared from the parents of the special-needs children. The principal wrote a short note back to the parent, explaining that the program would not sacrifice time for subject-matter concentration and would help all children understand each other better.

The program began on schedule. At first, the special-needs children didn't mingle well with the other children in free-choice situations, such as on the playground. Gradually, however, they were invited to join teams in the children's games. And at least once a week, the two special education teachers supervised a structured game in which the special-needs children and the other children participated in equal numbers. The teachers heard some taunting and snickering by the other children about the facial characteristics of two of the children who had Down's Syndrome. Nevertheless, during the science periods, the children from the regular class worked well with the special-needs children, who seemed to look forward to the experience. During the art classes, the two groups interacted much less, each pursuing their own artwork.

Three weeks after the integration program began, the principal received a telephone call from Mrs. Townsley, a parent of a child in the special-needs classroom, requesting an appointment to discuss the program in the presence of a friend, Mrs. Houtz, who was a parent of one of the children in the regular classes; she asked that the director of special education also be present. Eden agreed and before the meeting informed Tim Curtis about the latest events in the situation, including current activities and teachers' observations, which were quite positive.

During the appointment, Mrs. Townsley expressed a complete understanding of the reasons behind the integration program, but said, "My real concern is that these activities are taking time away from the real focus on the skills that the two special teachers were able to carry out before this program started. I don't think that our special children can afford the sacrifice of *any* time." Mrs. Houtz added, "It seems strange because of the difference between our children, but I have the same concern in the other direction. I think this new program is taking valuable time away from challenging my child, too. In addition (and I don't mean any offense to you, Elizabeth) but I think that sometimes if children who have normal potential see or work with children who have perhaps less potential, they may decide that they are fine as they are and don't need to work as hard anymore."

Tim Curtis explained to the parents the important philosophy behind integrating different kinds of children, and Eden repeated the rationale that she had explained in her original letters to parents before the program began. Mrs. Townsley replied, "Yes, I understand all those things, and I respect your professional point of view, but you need to understand that we are parents who are concerned about these valuable school years, and we feel that we cannot have our children participate in an experiment like this."

Mrs. Houtz then said, "I think you should know that we are not only speaking for ourselves but also for several other parents who have contacted us. So we're here to tell you that we wish to have the program either stopped or to allow parents of both classes a choice in the matter; we thought this would be a more reasonable approach than simply writing a letter to the superintendent and the chairman of the school board and asking that it be discussed in public."

There was a pause in the conversation. The principal and the director of special education looked at each other before responding to this last comment.

Discussion Questions

1. What would be the most appropriate statement for the educators in this situation to make at this moment in the meeting? Why?

2. If you were the director of special education in this situation, would you attempt to resolve this situation at this meeting, ask for another meeting later, or invite the parents to make their concerns known to the superintendent and the school board so that a full public discussion can take place?

3. What are the *real* concerns behind the *expressed* concerns of the parent of the special-needs child?

4. What are the *real* concerns behind the *expressed* concerns of the parent of the child from the regular classroom?

5. In what ways, if any, should the principal have acted differently before the program was implemented?

6. In what ways should the director of special education have acted differently before the program was implemented?

7. What are the positive and negative implications of permitting parents to have a *choice* in this program, as opposed to making it an all-or-nothing program?

8. If you were the director of special education and wanted to encourage the principal to *expand* this program to encompass other kinds of activities, in spite of parents' concerns, what types of expansion would you recommend?

9. What long-term plans would you make for the school district if you were the director of special education, in relation to integration activities for *other* special education classes?

Case Study 19

Compensatory Education Programs

Issue: Best use of restricted funds

For seven years the elementary schools in the Springfield School District had qualified for compensatory education funding under Chapter One of the federal Elementary and Secondary Education Act. Springfield's funding was specifically allocated for classroom instructional aides in grades 1-3. The district had a trained corps of instructional aides who were highly valued by the teachers they served and who, in effect, had reduced the adult-pupil ratio in the primary grades.

According to federal guidelines, only four of the seven schools qualified for Chapter One aid. However, the difference in the percentage of Springfield's families who were on "Aid to Families of Dependent Children" (AFDC)—the criterion used for determining the target schools—varied up or down each year by only a few percentage points from the required minimum of 3 percent. In fact, the percentage of AFDC children across the seven schools ranged from a low of 2 percent to a high of 6 percent. Thus, although technically only four of the seven schools could legally be designated as target schools in order to receive federal funds, the actual need was general across the school district and varied even from year to year when only a few families moved in or out of a school boundary area.

Consequently, for the past three years, the school principals, in a consensus agreement with Superintendent Chan Lim, had divided the funding equally across *all* schools in order to provide each grade 1-3 classroom in the district with an instructional aide. When the funding application was prepared each year for the federal government, only the target schools were identified and listed in the application. In any three-year period, because of the mobility of families, every school at one time or another appeared on the legally qualified list, although it was never possible in any single year to *technically* claim that all schools satisfied the criterion of 3 percent or more of children on AFDC.

A representative from the state department of education was scheduled to visit the school district to carry out a regular compliance check in terms of the federal grant under Chapter One—to ensure that funds were being expended completely and properly. The school district believed that it had a totally justifiable reason for equal distribution of the funds, but it was also technically out of compliance with the law.

The compliance officer first visited that year's target schools and was satisfied that the classroom aides were indeed providing appropriate help to the children. In some cases, the target children were not from families on AFDC but had special education needs independent of their socioeconomic level.

When the compliance officer visited the district office to audit the expenditure of federal funds, she of course discovered that the funds were distributed over *all* schools, not solely to the target schools for that year. She regretfully told Superintendent Lim that she would have to report the district's failure to comply and would place a temporary stop on the expenditure of federal funds until the situation was changed in some appropriate way.

Two weeks later, to no one's surprise, a copy of the compliance officer's report arrived on Lim's desk. The superintendent immediately conferred with the director of curriculum to decide on an appropriate step to take. It was clear that the federal funds had to be used for instructional aides, since the district didn't have enough money for them. The teachers, hearing a rumor that classroom aides would be laid off, immediately wrote to the superintendent protesting that aides were essential to proper instruction in the primary grades. The Parents' Association president filed a similarly strong letter supporting the aides.

However, the state department of education report had the force of law. Lim and his curriculum director and district financial officer made an immediate appointment with the federal funds distribution officer to discuss an exception to the federal ruling.

Discussion Questions

1. If you accept the rationale for equal distribution of these funds based on the small range of difference in percentage of AFDC families across the school district, what arguments would you recommend that Superintendent Lim and his staff present when they meet with the federal officer?

2. If federal guidelines prohibit funds for schools having less than 3 percent AFDC children, what other strategies might the district use in the future to provide service to these children *and* maintain compliance with federal guidelines?

3. In what ways is the action of the district administrators ethical and unethical in trying to circumvent these explicit federal guidelines?

4. Suppose you are the superintendent in this situation. What kind of report would you make to the next meeting of the school board when information is given to them about this ruling by the compliance officer?

5. If you were able to rewrite the federal guidelines for the Chapter One program, how would you prevent this kind of dilemma for this kind of school district in the future?

Group V.
Cases in the
Evaluation of
Curriculum

This final section offers three cases depicting the interaction of evaluation and curriculum and its effects on administrators, teachers, parents, and students. Important considerations are raised about who evaluates, what should be evaluated, and how evaluation should be interpreted and used in a school district. Since evaluation is a subject of growing interest in U.S. schools today, how would you, as a curriculum leader, define this interaction and answer the questions raised?

Case Study 20

State Testing Programs

Issue: What measures should be used to determine what students are learning, and how should they be interpreted?

Superintendent Clem Robinson was notified by the State Department of Education that the Possum Hollow School District would be part of a new annual statewide testing program in grades 3, 7, and 10. The first test would be administered next October. Robinson called his director of instruction, Susan Schiller, into his office and discussed with her the set of sample test items that came with the notification.

Schiller and Robinson found that the items assessed student performance in reading comprehension, mathematical computation, and use of appropriate grammar—all in a multiple-choice format.

The comprehension items in the reading portion of the test also provided multiple-choice answers to questions about written paragraphs on nonfiction topics. Schiller said that the reading level on all portions of the test appeared to be at roughly the median level for the Possum Hollow School District. She noted that the items partially resembled the items on a commercially produced test that the district administered each year in grades 2, 4, and 6.

With the district psychologist, who had a strong background in statistics, the director of instruction went through the results and noticed that the district mean scores in reading were at the 75th percentile rank for the state; the math mean score was at the 80th percentile statewide; and the writing (grammar) score was at the 69th percentile. These results were comparable to some extent with the district mean scores on a *national* percentile rank in the commercial test the district gave annually. The rank for that test at each of the grade levels ranged between the 60th and 70th percentile among the three subtest areas.

Schiller started to write the report that she would present to the school board at its next regular meeting. She prepared overhead transparencies showing both the statewide results for the district as well as the earlier results on a national basis in the commercially published test. She also included sample questions from the original enclosure in the announcement from the State Department of Education, so the board could see the types of test items that were given.

On the evening of the board meeting, Schiller made her presentation by explaining the background of the test, the types of items, the frequency of testing, the amount of classroom time used by the testing, and the percentile results of the district mean scores on both the state test and the commercially published test. She then invited questions from board members.

Six of the nine board members were uninterested in the results, but three were eager to ask questions. The first said, "I'm surprised that we didn't do better in reading compared with the other districts in the state. After all, we spent considerable money last year to bring in an inservice trainer for our teachers in reading, and our graduates go on to the state university in good numbers every year. Why is this?"

Before Schiller could reply, a second board member interjected, "Before you answer that question, I must say that I can't understand why our math scores aren't right up near the top, considering that last year we adopted those new materials that emphasize lots of creative thinking in math problem solving, beginning in the early grades. Have we been wasting our money and time?"

Schiller started to explain that the statewide test assessed only a portion of the curriculum in the subject areas it tested, and that the results of the inservice training in reading and the new math materials might not ever show on this type of test. She added that because the test was in its first year of administration, there would probably be some revisions to eliminate items that were not good discriminators of achievement, and that she would be glad to come back to the board's next meeting with further details on the test in relation to the district curriculum.

The third interested board member then said, "I look forward to that next report, because there's no question that we can do better, and I want to see us right up in the 90th percentile next year."

Superintendent Robinson said he would be glad to work with the director of instruction and others to prepare a more detailed report for the next meeting. He agreed that it would be useful and important for all teachers to work to improve scores in those three subject areas.

On the way out of the meeting at the end of the evening, the vice president of the district PTA approached Schiller and said, "We must be doing better than those tests show; I know a lot of parents will be interested in more explanation at the next meeting."

The following morning, Schiller sat down at her desk to develop a full interpretation of the test, as well as an explanation to give the school board at its next meeting.

Discussion Questions

1. What issues in education and politics are illustrated by the questions asked by the school board members?

2. In what ways might teacher attitude toward the tests have affected the results? What should be done about that?

3. If you were the director of instruction, how would you try to interpret test results like these to a *lay* audience?

4. Would it be possible to provide a more complete evaluation model for the district, to accompany the state test results, so that the community can understand more fully all that the curriculum is trying to accomplish? How?

6. Write an outline of the report the director of instruction should prepare for the next school board meeting.

Case Study 21

The Impact of Teacher Evaluation Practices on Innovation

Issue: How to avoid trivializing teacher evaluation

For the last two years, Pelham Superintendent Joan Shell had hired school principals whom she expected to be open to new curriculum ideas and eager to improve the educational process. She had also hired a new curriculum director, John Amis. Amis had a good reputation as a seasoned, level-headed professional who had developed successful curriculum programs in other districts.

In addition, the district's teachers had participated in a series of workshops on several curriculum innovations, particularly in methods of affective development and in several of the newer problem-solving, thinking skill programs.

John Amis started his work by consulting with teachers and administrators on what they saw as the district's curriculum needs and then formed curriculum committees of teachers. Each committee was responsible for one subject area and met regularly once a week. Each committee also had a "shadow" companion committee of other teachers who would react to the work of the committee and raise questions for clarification. Since they were involved in all of these committees, as a group the teachers felt a sense of ownership, enthusiasm, and cooperation. Every teacher knew something of what was being done within all committees.

The superintendent and the school board accepted and encouraged this work. Relations between administrators and teachers were no longer adversarial; a cooperative spirit had developed, with all parties giving students top priority. Principals sent newsletters to parents to regularly inform them about progress in the curriculum revision and trends in student achievement. And the annual survey mailed to parents indicated high parent satisfaction with school personnel.

However, not every school district in the state was moving forward as smoothly and progressively in curriculum revision as was Pelham. In fact, legislators who had children in other less progressive school districts became a target for lobbyists who represented parents promoting a stringent law for teacher evaluation using student test scores. Teachers in Pelham, learning of the new law, began to fear that their efforts in developing student character and thinking skills would not be recognized under the new law because virtually no available tests could demonstrate student achievement in those areas. The Pelham teachers called a special meeting to discuss the issue of teacher evaluation. Three of the most respected teachers expressed some widely held sentiments:

"Why should we work hard for long hours trying to build character and in the end only be held responsible for how much the students achieve on paper-and-pencil tests?"

"I've been working with slow learners. Does this mean I'm a bad teacher because my students don't achieve as quickly or as much as other students?"

"Shouldn't we consider going back to lower skill achievement objectives so that we can assure ourselves of better evaluation? I have a family to support, after all."

These and other questions were raised. Since the teachers knew how to write behavioral objectives and were familiar with Bloom's taxonomy of cognitive objectives, they soon developed a set of new objectives at the lowest skill levels.

During the first year of the new state teacher evaluation law, the Pelham District Teacher Evaluation Committee began to collect teacher evaluation forms from neighboring districts to compare procedures. To their surprise, they found that the other districts had included on their forms such descriptors as: "The classroom has a warm atmosphere" and "The teacher is friendly." The teachers pressed the Pelham district administrators to adopt this type of item for their evaluation form, even though everyone—teachers, administrators, superintendent, and parents—recognized that these subjective items would render teacher evaluation meaningless. Rather than moving toward continuous improvement, such an evaluation system would become only routine low-level paperwork for both teachers and administrators.

Alarmed, John Amis met with Superintendent Shell, who, in turn, discussed the issue with principals. Teachers defended their position, saying that since evaluation was based only on achievement, they were not ready to "stick their necks out" by trying new approaches to instruction and would instead work toward student achievement in basic subject areas to assure themselves of "good" evaluations.

The word about the teachers' position spread around the community. Parents became very concerned, and the school board faced a dilemma. On the one hand, board members wanted the district to satisfy the law; on the other hand, they wanted the tea   to continue their previously exciting work with students in the new curriculum.

Superintendent Shell called another administrators' meeting to reexamine the issue. John Amis, the assistant superintendent, the principals, teachers' representatives, and the chairman of the board all attended. Everyone seemed to want to find a solution to the issue. During the discussion, Amis raised the question, "What would happen if we were to develop *two* systems: the first to satisfy the letter of the law on lower-level measurable objectives, and a second optional system that will be based on some experimental items on higher problem-solving skills and individual student affective growth?" There was silence for an interminable minute. Shell noted some interest and said, "We need to figure out whether or not this is a feasible approach."

Discussion Questions

1. How could the negative teacher reaction in Pelham have been prevented when the new evaluation law was passed?

2. What is your opinion of John Amis's suggestion of a dual evaluation system?

3. If you were Amis, how would you develop such a dual system?

4. What problems of implementation of a dual system would need to be solved?

5. Which problems would be most difficult to solve?

6. What criteria would you suggest for evaluating teachers that would also demonstrate the improvements in district curriculum that had been achieved *prior* to the new law?

Case Study 22

The Outside Consultant

Issue: Pros and cons of the outsider's point of view

Sue Ellsworth, with five years of experience as a curriculum administrator, was hired to be Washington County's first curriculum director. Her initial task in this small, eight-school district was to meet with teachers and administrators to find out what was happening in district programs and to ask for their perceptions of needs for improvement.

After interviewing the faculty at two schools, Ellsworth began to see a pattern: Teachers were dissatisfied because there had been some kind of change in the district's curriculum every year for the past five years. They also complained about having to develop written objectives for each school day with no or very little training in that area. The principals in the district had another problem they tried to hide: They had little knowledge of and interest in instructional improvement.

Ellsworth found that the principals as a group also had few ideas about how to assert educational leadership in their schools, although they had many ideas about school discipline, PTA fund raising, and athletic competitions. When asked what the job of a principal should be, one principal replied, "Three things—smooth administrative procedures, control of students, and keeping parents happy." Another principal said, "Our responsibilities are and have been primarily to prepare and administer the budget, sign letters to parents when their children are late or absent, respond quickly to telephone questions from the central office or parents, call staff meetings to convey messages from the central office, make sure that teachers are punctual, and reserve at least 15 minutes every day to walk through the corridors of the school to get a quick overview of student behavior."

Ellsworth then called a principals' meeting to talk about some of her ideas regarding educational reform and the integrated curriculum, the differences between supervision and evaluation, and computer-assisted instruction. Thirty minutes later, the stony-faced silence of the principals clearly showed their alienation. Not one of the principals offered a single question or opinion.

In obvious frustration, she then met with the superintendent and assistant superintendent and recommended an in-depth evaluation of all educational programs, starting with the elementary schools. In a meeting with the principals, the superintendent proposed a district-wide curriculum evaluation and received their tacit approval. The superintendent then called a meeting of all elementary school teachers. They warmly welcomed the idea of discussing curriculum on a districtwide basis, subject by subject. At the end of the first meeting, three teachers said to Ellsworth, "This kind of a meeting has been long overdue in the district."

Noting possible conflicts between principals and teachers, Ellsworth suggested that an outside consultant become the major curriculum evaluator. Joe Claxton, a respected professor of program evaluation from nearby Lincoln University, agreed to carry out this work. He was known as a person who could easily relate to people and who had done several other school district evaluations; he had proven technical ability. He came to the district office for a preliminary meeting to discuss the evaluation plan with the administrators, curriculum director, and teacher representatives. The topics he raised included the purposes of evaluation in schools; resources for evaluation (staff time, secretarial support, funding, materials); the role of school decision-making in evaluation; and the amount of time allotted for his evaluation.

Everyone present seemed comfortable with Claxton and expressed confidence in him. His evaluation design called for analyzing the district's printed curriculum guides, teachers' skills, student achievement and background, materials used in classrooms, and administrative practices relating to instruction.

Claxton's evaluation took about a year. When his final report was complete, he presented his findings to the superintendent, her assistant, and Sue Ellsworth. The report showed that the district's programs were deficient in terms of completeness and articulation, in the regular supervision of teachers, and in principals' support for program coordination.

School principals and representative teachers discussed the report in detail at a special meeting. The rather negative results seemed to cause much discomfort among the principals. They privately expressed to each other that the new curriculum director seemed to be "out to get us." "Where did they get that curriculum director?" asked one. "She doesn't know how schools are *really* run." Another asked, "Is she here to tell *us* what to do?"

The majority of the teachers, however, welcomed the report's findings and circulated a petition among district faculty calling for administrative help to improve instruction. The teachers' comments were favorable: "It is about *time* to examine our curriculum!" "How interesting to find someone like Sue Ellsworth, who talks to us as professionals." "I wish we had had someone like Sue a long time ago." There were four dissenting teachers who said that the evaluation was "too harsh" and that teachers deserved "better treatment as hardworking professionals."

Then the report reached the school board. Three board members said that they had read the report with dismay, and had been unaware of such deficiencies in the district programs. Two other members then publicly praised the evaluator's efforts and asked the superintendent for a plan of remediation. The local newspaper reported on the special meeting.

The following day, a delegation of eight parents (all PTA officers) made an appointment to see the superintendent and Sue Ellsworth together in the district office.

Discussion Questions

1. What should Sue Ellsworth expect to hear from the parents at this meeting? How should she reply?

2. What should she tell the parents about the plan for next steps in the district?

3. Do you agree or disagree with Sue Ellsworth's decision to use an outside evaluator? Why?

4. If you had been the curriculum director in this case, what would you have done about program evaluation immediately after your arrival on the job?

5. List at least three suggestions for improving the curriculum leadership behavior of the district principals.

6. What would be the most appropriate action for the superintendent to take in regard to the principals?

7. There are many progressive principals today who are also educational leaders. What are three or four characteristic behaviors of the principal who is *also* an educational leader?

8. How would you as a curriculum director foster that kind of behavior in principals in your district?

Appendix

Summary of Issues

I. Cases in Curriculum Development

Case Study 1. The School Board and Curriculum from the Top Down
The school board opposes a teacher-developed revision of the social studies curriculum, fearing that students won't be able to learn enough basics about world history.

Case Study 2. Teachers' Power in Deciding Curriculum
Teachers oppose a new English curriculum proposed by the school board and district curriculum committee; they claim that the district shouldn't determine curriculum—teachers should.

Case Study 3. The Parents Association and the Curriculum Agenda
Community members object to a districtwide program of sex/AIDs education initiated by the superintendent. The citizens feel that such information should be provided to students by their parents and clergymen.

Case Study 4. The State and the Local District
The junior high principal objects to new curriculum guides developed by the state department of education. The district's director of curriculum plans to administer competency tests based on those state guides, which the principal feels are not as good as the program he has developed. He asks that his school be exempt.

Case Study 5. Professional and Community Factions Around Instructional Methods
Teachers serving on a districtwide social studies curriculum committee disagree on the purpose and focus for a new program. Who should decide?

II. Cases in Curriculum Implementation

Case Study 6. Developing Professional Enthusiasm
The director of curriculum and the superintendent want to give teachers release time away from classrooms for inservice on current teaching methods. The PTA objects, saying teachers should work on self-improvement on their own time and spend their work time in the classroom.

Case Study 7. Assessing Curriculum Change
Teachers and students are enthusiastic about the new science curriculum, but after the first year of implementation, tests show no significant increase in student achievement. The principal needs to give the superintendent solid reasons for not throwing out the new program and returning to the old.

Case Study 8. Curriculum Materials: Which Criteria to Use
When the high school math department needed to update its curriculum, it chose new textbooks in algebra and then revised the curriculum guide to correspond to the content sequence of the new textbooks.

Case Study 9. Finding "Room" for Thinking Skills

A group of teachers who participated in a workshop on thinking skills find that their department heads are more concerned about getting through the prescribed curriculum than teaching thinking skills to students. The district has given no support to the teaching of thinking skills, and they have not been formally recognized in curriculum guides.

III. Cases in Personnel and Curriculum

Case Study 10. Conflict of Interest

A special education teacher who moonlights for a local clinic has recommended that some of his students use the services of the clinic. But is that clinic really the best choice, or was it recommended because the teacher wants to help the clinic's business?

Case Study 11. Teacher Work Stoppage

When teachers go on strike, the district curriculum developer is torn between loyalty to the teachers with whom she works and loyalty to the administration, her employer. She must take a side, but in doing so, who will she alienate and how seriously will that hurt her effectiveness?

Case Study 12. Textbook Selection Policies and Procedures

The district's textbook selection committee recommends several proposed textbooks that the school board rejects on the basis of "inside" information from a member of the committee who is privately working against the committee's efforts. The committee member is eventually reprimanded—but was that reprimand ethical, and, more fundamentally, have all the parties played their roles appropriately?

Case Study 13. Teacher Curricular Autonomy

An outsider who was recently hired to be the new curriculum coordinator finds that her efforts to revise the language arts curriculum are being undermined by a high school teacher (among others) who disagrees with her progressive ideas and who seems to hold a grudge at having lost his own bid for the coordinator's job.

Case Study 14. Staffing for Curriculum Leadership

A district that had once been financially stable faces economic problems when the town's major industry closes down. The school board has authorized the superintendent to make major budget cuts, but to ensure that class sizes don't increase.

Case Study 15. The Budget Squeeze

The district's parent-teacher committee is trying to decide where to make some needed budget cuts. The teachers on the committee oppose program and faculty cuts; the parents recommend cutting back on teachers of home economics, physical education, industrial arts, driver education, art, and music. When parents in the community are polled, they agree with the parent members of the committee, and the school board accepts their recommendation.

IV. Cases in Programs for Special Populations

Case Study 16. An Influx of Immigrants

Should non-English-speaking immigrant children be pulled from their regular classes for instruction in their own language? The immigrant parents say yes, the Teachers Association says no. The director of instruction is asked to make a recommendation based on what is educationally best for the students.

Case Study 17.   Mainstreaming

The school district must come up with a plan for educating hearing-impaired Emily, who is having difficulty learning and adjusting to life in the regular classroom, where the teacher has had little background in special education. How can the district do what the law requires (educate in the least restrictive environment) and provide what is best for Emily's special situation?

Case Study 18.   Concerns of Parents of Mainstreamed vs. Nonhandicapped Children

An elementary school allots time for handicapped and nonhandicapped children to work and play together, an enriching experience for both groups of students. But parents of both groups are concerned that the program takes time away from more important skills their children need.

Case Study 19.   Compensatory Education Program

The school district is given federal funds for use only in schools with the largest percentage of needy children. Since there are needy children in all the schools, however, the district has been spreading the funds around. Now the district is facing the loss its federal funds unless it complies with the law; but this means its education program will suffer.

V.   Cases in the Evaluation of Curriculum

Case Study 20.   State Testing Program

The district's students haven't performed up to expectations on a new state testing program. District administrators feel that the test items were not particularly good and the results not meaningful. Now they must explain this to school board members and parents who believe there must be something wrong with the district's instructional program.

Case Study 21.   The Impact of Teacher Evaluation Practices on Innovation

The state has passed a law requiring stringent teacher evaluation. Teachers in a progressive district, fearing they'll be judged on inappropriate criteria, recommend watering down the teacher evaluation forms, as other districts have done, to make them look good and to enable them to keep working on the worthwhile goals they've already set for their students. Yet everyone recognizes that this proposal would make teacher evaluation a sham.

Case Study 22.   The Outside Consultant

The new curriculum director finds that the district's principals are slack, and teachers are disgruntled with the lack of strong leadership. An outside consultant is hired to appraise the situation and to serve as the "bad guy" when the principals hear the negative findings. Now the curriculum director has to deal with the principals and the public, who will want to know how the situation will be improved.